*Reflections on a Rural Childhood*

# Reflections on a Rural Childhood

G. Alan Brooks

Copyright © 2011 by G. Alan Brooks.

Library of Congress Control Number: 2011912187
ISBN: Hardcover 978-1-4653-3684-2
Softcover 978-1-4653-3683-5
Ebook 978-1-4653-3685-9

All rights reserved. No part of this book may be reproduced or transmitted in any form or by any means, electronic or mechanical, including photocopying, recording, or by any information storage and retrieval system, without permission in writing from the copyright owner.

This book was printed in the United States of America.

**To order additional copies of this book, contact:**
Xlibris Corporation
1-888-795-4274
www.Xlibris.com
Orders@Xlibris.com
100535

For my family and friends who have enriched my life.

"If you don't go, you won't know."
Old Brooks Family Saying

This is a tale of times past. It is a nostalgic reflection and a walk down memory lane. The chapters are more or less in chronological order, but occasionally, there might be some exceptions when stories are close in time. These reflections are not endorsements of any particular way of life.

Our country was rural in the beginning of its development and has become ever more urban as time has passed. Greater parts of our population now live in urban areas, and fewer and fewer family farms are still in production. The sustenance farmers and families who live on and work the land have almost disappeared. The need to hunt for food is certainly a thing of the past.

A few of my cousins, aunts, and distant relatives still live on and around of what was once "the farm." However, my immediate family members all live in large urban areas and are business people, technology entrepreneurs, doctors, artists, lawyers, and investment bankers. For those who live in the city, I wanted to leave behind some stories about my rural childhood and a way of life that once existed not so long ago. These reflections take place from my early childhood until my graduation from high school (1940–1958).

Note: The images and photos are the closest I could find to create the feeling of each story. Many are actual photos of people who are included in the story while some images were found by searching the internet. Therefore, few images are not of the real Brooks family members or the precise area discussed in these stories.

What I have written is true, mainly.

# Introduction

"Wow, is the wind blowing hard." In 1945, a strong hurricane moved along the coast of Florida and came ashore at Cedar Key. On the farm, it gave us some extremely powerful winds that created a lot of locally heavy rainfall, flooding, and property damage. In those days, our area was sparsely populated. There were no storm shelters for the citizens to use when a hurricane was blowing.

My father owned a farm with about six hundred acres of land, which included a farmhouse, a barn, and a rock gas station that faced Highway 41. I do not remember all the financial details, but a few years earlier, Grandpa Brooks had given the farm to my father along with the mortgage. The station was built from rocks removed from the cultivated land around the farm, and it was one of the strongest buildings in the area. In fact, it is still standing sixty-five years later and continues to be in good shape.

The wind was incredibly strong, and I remember being put on a table to keep my feet and pants from getting wet since the water was pouring in under the front door of the station. There must have been fifty people crowded together inside the small rock building. Many were Brooks families, and while there was concern about the howling weather outside, the laughter, eating, singing, and joking is a fond memory. At that moment, I believed our farm and our family made this little community called Montbrook. Florida, the safest and the best place in the world to live.

# Chapter One

"Alan, where are you?" It was Easter Sunday, and we were dressed in our finest clothes, especially me. My new white Easter suit was the result of an unusual splurge by my mother, Rubye. It consisted of a pair of crisp white pants, a beautifully pleated shirt, and a white coat. As a five-year-old, the excitement about my new suit was somewhat lost on me.

While the rest of the family—my father, my mother, and my older sister—were loading the pickup truck with food for the picnic after church, I ran to the barn to play. I found a dead rat, which had just been killed by one of our many barn cats, and did as I had been taught to do. I threw the rat into the garbage pail, which was outside of the barn. Right next to the garbage pail was a discarded, almost empty grease bucket used to grease our farm implements. I am not sure why, but I decided to crawl into the grease bucket and hide from the family.

This is where they found me after about twenty minutes of hunting and repeatedly calling my name. True to a good hider, I made no noise and no movement. Johnny, one of the family dogs, gave me away.

My new suit was ruined, and the excitement and extra cost, which had given my mother so much pleasure, were lost in a quick moment of disappointed surprise. An old black-and-white photo taken at that moment by my sister, Jo Ann, is one of my first childhood memories. Thankfully, it does not show the expression on my mother's face.

# Chapter Two

"Baker and Alan are American sailors just like Uncle Joe." In a couple of faded photographs, Baker and I are dressed in our new white sailor suits and headed to Mema's for a huge dinner along with our parents. The war was raging in the Pacific, and our uncle Joe, my father's younger brother, was a sailor on one of the naval vessels.

The Japanese had bombed Pearl Harbor, and our government had made a formal declaration of war only a few days earlier. Everyone was both concerned about his safety and proud that Uncle Joe was serving our country. My memories of this time are those that were repeatedly told to me since I was just over a year old. However, those days were worrisome times for my grandparents, parents, uncles, and aunts.

They quickly turned into tragic days when just a few weeks later, the government reported the death of Uncle Joe. Grandpa Brooks was extremely devastated by his son's death. Uncle Joe had been a favorite of all who knew him. He had perished in a faraway place, defending our country, and he would not be forgotten. When I was old enough to understand war, my grandfather said to me, "The idiocy of war, the lunacy of war." As I have grown older, I can see he was right, but unfortunately, there seems to be no way to stop it.

I am on the right in the photo on the left, and I am in the picture on the right.

# Chapter Three

"Momma, it hurts." At the community doctor's office, we waited for more than one hour while my left leg was bleeding more than a little. I remember my mother pressing a towel on the cut and telling me not to worry as the blood dripped onto the linoleum floor in the cheaply furnished office.

Just a short while before this, I had been helping our hired hand, Ernest, gather a load of peanuts from the front forty. Ernest was driving the old Ford 8N tractor and pulling a flatbed trailer loaded with around fifty burlap bags of peanuts. The front forty had two gates, one on the north end and one on the south end.

We had entered through the south gate, and since there were no animals in the field, we had left the south gate open to avoid the need to reopen it when we were ready to leave. I do not know why Ernest picked the north gate as the one we needed to use to return to the barn, but the north gate was closed. I was riding on the front edge of the trailer on two-hundred-pound bags of peanuts. As we approached the gate, I wanted to be helpful, so I decided to run ahead and open the gate for Ernest.

The front forty was a super sandy field, and the heavy load of the peanuts dug deep into the sand and made ruts maybe six inches deep. The trailer had two wheels, one on each side, but there were no tires on the wheels, only rims, which saved my father money. As I jumped from the trailer, I slipped under the right wheel with my left leg extended. The trailer passed over my leg, right next to my groin, and the rim made a severe cut. Everyone says I was lucky that it did not cut my leg off completely, but I guess I have always been quite lucky.

Anyway, the doctor sewed up the cut; I went back to the farm and spent the rest of the day getting a lot of attention from my mother, Mema, and Jo Ann. Mother made a delicious blackberry doobie as a special treat for her suffering six-year-old son.

# Chapter Four

"I see the deer." We were racing through the dense, vine-tangled woods on Lady, a spirited quarter horse. My father, Bob, was in the saddle, and I was riding behind him as we followed the dogs, which were chasing the deer.

We could occasionally see white flashes of the deer's tail. We had caught a clean glance of the deer when the dogs jumped him from a palmetto thicket, and we knew it was a fair-sized buck. We were about one hundred yards behind the deer when he ran through a small pond in an attempt to elude the dogs by using the water to hide his scent.

The pond was only a few feet deep, but Lady had to slow down a little as we entered the water. It was a good thing because, at that moment, my father saw the deer, threw up his gun to shoot, fired the gun twice, and caused Lady to buck me off. It was unusually cold that morning, and when I hit the water, I think I lost my breath for few seconds. The tree where I hit my head was not too large, and I am sure it somewhat bent with the blow. As a result, I was soaking wet with a big knot on my head, and making matters worse, my father had missed the deer.

He said it was because I grabbed his arm as I was falling. I am not sure that my falling and grabbing were the real reasons he missed, but the memory of a seven-year-old is not so reliable. In any event, we did not have deer meat for dinner that night, and we had to settle for Spam sandwiches with lettuce, tomato, and mayonnaise. If you have not tried Spam, you have missed a treat.

Another snack, not currently eaten by my immediate family, is Vienna sausage that we carried in our hunting jackets along with saltine crackers to eat during the day.

# Chapter Five

"Kids, we are moving to town." Williston, Florida, was a small community with a population of around one thousand only four miles from the farm. I was only six or seven years old when Daddy lost the farm that had been part of the Brooks land for years.

He just could not keep up with the mortgage payments, so he sold the land to Jack Frasier. He stopped full-time farming a few years earlier, and he took a job with the Florida Fish and Wildlife Conservation Commission as a ranger. Prior to selling his land, my dad, Uncle Oliver, Uncle Everett, and Uncle Burke all together had about three thousand five hundred acres of land that was settled by my great-grandfather, Montholon Brooks.

Montholon and his parents were original Florida pioneers, who came to Florida in the same oxcart train as Osceola and his mother around 1815. A few years after their arrival, Osceola became the most famous Seminole Indian chief of all-time, and our family was always friendly with the Seminole tribe, especially Chief Micanopy of the Alachua Seminoles. We actually have a few Indians buried on their horses in our family graveyard. I have always been ashamed at the deceit used by the army to capture Osceola and the way he died and how his remains were treated. My cousin, Butch, has an impressive arrowhead collection that he picked up from the fields on our land.

Although we lost our farm, I still spent most of my free time with my uncles, aunts, and cousins on their land. I could walk to the farm from town when there was no ride available. I have always called the land owned by my uncles and aunts "the farm" and think of myself as one raised on a farm. As of this writing, only Aunt Louise, Baker, and a grandson of Uncle Burke have kept their land largely intact. The rest of the land has vanished to be occupied by strangers from another world. The original Brooks landscape is truly gone with the wind.

# Chapter Six

"Look out below. Here I come." The tree was around fifty feet tall, and the small platform someone had built was probably thirty feet up the tree. It was necessary to climb around twenty steps built by nailing two-by-fours to the trunk of the tree. The platform itself was four two-by-fours nailed together, and it had no bounce.

It was over the small blue sinkhole we called Wekiva Springs, and only the bravest of us would dive from this platform into the narrow space below. I had only dived once before and had truly made an embarrassing belly flop. This time I was determined to make a better dive. Our little league baseball team had come to the springs to swim and have a picnic with our coach. It had taken all of my courage to go back up the tree, and I yelled to all below to watch as I dived from the tree. Ed Barton must not have heard my yells because just as I dived, he made a running jump from the shore into the same spot as I was headed.

The next thing I remember was Coach Durrance asking me if I could hear him. They told me that I had been unconscious for several minutes. I apparently hit my head on Ed's elbow, and it crushed my skull and created a soft spot like the one you can feel on babies. The soft spot lasted for about two years, and many people thought they could feel my brain while they joked I might not have one.

# Chapter Seven

Drucilla Newsom

"Alan, come over, and let's play." Drucilla was calling my name from her backyard. Our parents were playing penny-ante poker at her house with some other friends.

Her dad was a farmer like my father but more successful and well respected in the community. After losing our farm, we were neighbors in a mixed neighborhood in town, and the backyard of our rented house shared a common lot line with their impressive home.

My father was an excellent cardplayer when he was sober, and my mother loved cards of all kinds. Years later when Mother was severely afflicted with Alzheimer's, she could still play a fairly decent game of bridge with her sisters who would visit each Saturday for years to give her as much pleasure as one can have with Alzheimer's.

Drucilla wanted to play monopoly, and we genuinely liked the game and the idea that if you were clever with real estate, there was money to be made and a game to win. Often we played monopoly for hours while waiting for our parents to finish their poker game. If they let us stay up until they finished, we had the fun of looking under the poker table where they would always leave a few pennies, nickels, and dimes for us to find and use at the movies for nine-cent popcorns and nickel Cokes.

Drucilla was my best friend for years, and we shared many youthful moments and childhood events as we went to the same elementary and high school together. In fact, we were both leads in our junior and senior high school plays. She was a cheerleader. I played football and basketball, and we were both in the band. We were on the same school bus for many road trips, and while we were never romantically involved, I always tried to look out for her and she for me.

# Chapter Eight

"Daddy, let's go home." Losing the farm was a real downer for Daddy. He tried many different ways to make a living: a ranger with the wildlife commission, a part owner of a produce shed, a fruit shop owner, a fertilizer-spreading operator, and finally, a mechanic.

"Let's go home" was a frequent plea of mine when he got drunk and would not leave Pete Golden's bar. I can truly say that these were some of the most embarrassing and stressful moments in my life. He would often make fun of my pleas and say mean things to me in front of the men in the bar. I learned from this experience that the judgment of the authority figure is not always correct.

We lived in town, in different rented homes, with the level of comfort slowly going down and down. Mother would send me into the bar after waiting hours for him to come home. He was totally different when drinking than when sober, and as I grew up, he was drunk more and more often. He was polite, smart, and caring when sober but a mean drunk. When he was drinking, he would abuse all of us, both verbally and physically.

The fear of what was going to happen when he came home was overshadowed by the fear that he would spend all of our limited money on whiskey if he stayed at the bar. The stress placed on our family by his drinking, lack of work, lack of income, wasting money needed for basics on whiskey, abusiveness, embarrassment in the community, and overall failure to provide a safe home was almost unbelievably difficult to accept.

Later, as I was graduating from high school, Mother could take no more, and she left him. She moved to Jacksonville with Sara and Robbie to move near Jo Ann, who was living there. He later followed her to Jacksonville, but the days of a rural life were essentially over for our immediate family.

# Chapter Nine

"Boy, I am hungry." I could think about nothing but eating my sandwich, and thankfully, the position of the sun indicated it was about noontime. I had been plowing one of Uncle Oliver's peanut fields all morning. I had been waiting almost from the moment I left our house to eat the steak and tomato sandwich that mother had made for me.

Breakfast had been around 5:30 a.m., and I had been alone on the tractor for about six hours just thinking about eating lunch under one of the massive Spanish oak trees on the edge of the field, where we had the water trough for the cows and a lot of shade. Butch was plowing in another field, and we were going to have lunch together and jawboning all kinds of stories as we usually did. While I did not have a watch, we all knew how to tell time by looking at the sun. We were keenly aware of the compass directions of north, south, east, and west. So we could put a stick in the ground, make a sundial in the sand, and tell time within thirty minutes with considerable accuracy.

We were too far from the farmhouse for someone to tell us when it was time to eat, so we made those decisions on our own. I decided it was time, and sure enough, as I drove the tractor over to the shade trees, I saw Butch coming to join me. We were talking, joking, and laughing as I pulled my sandwich out of my brown paper bag, and without looking, I took an enormous bite. I tasted the foulest piece of steak ever eaten by a human. It was grainy and slimly, and I vomited immediately.

When I calmed down, I looked closely at the sandwich, and it was not steak at all. It was *liver*. It was a calf's liver, which is almost the only thing to this day that I cannot eat. My family would eat all parts of almost any animal, but for some reason, I cannot eat liver. It just does not seem right to me.

# Chapter Ten

"Uncle Oliver, can we go to KP Hole today after work?" The Rainbow River was around fifteen miles from the farm, and boy, it was beautiful! The water was as clear as the sky and quite chilly at seventy-three degrees. The bank of the river at KP Hole was a beautiful white sand with BBQ grills scattered around the property. It was a public beach and open to all.

During the summer, many of the family children including Robbie, Sara, Jerry, Butch, Baker, Terry, Nanada, and me loved to go swimming in the river. Uncle Oliver, and sometimes my parents, would take us to KP Hole in a pickup truck. We would all be in the back of the truck with the most gleeful exuberance of singing, laughing, and storytelling while often drinking a strawberry soda and eating some cakes or moon pies.

The wind would be blowing in our faces, and our hair would be utterly tousled and wild.

Once we got to the river, we would run to the water to swim and look for turtles, fish, snakes, and all types of birds and even gators. A few of the richer families had boats with water skis. Frequently, they would invite us to ski or take a boat ride. The Rainbow River is around six miles long, and I think it is one of the most beautiful stretches of water in America with a clarity never seen in other rivers. It has a current of three to four knots, and we often floated down the river using inner tubes. We were picked up in Dunnellon a few hours after we left the beach at KP Hole by our parents.

In later years, the students from the University of Florida would come over to float down the river with beer and music. But when I was a kid, we never drank nor played music on the river because the natural beauty of the area and our enthusiastic youth were intoxicating orchestras by themselves.

# Chapter Eleven

"Butch, you go first," I told my cousin as we pulled up to Lawton Hole. There are many sinkholes in Central Florida caused by the weak limestone strata that sometimes collapses into the underground aquifer.

Lawton Hole was named after Ole Man Lawton, who got drunk one night and drove his team of horses into the sinkhole and was never found; only the tracks of his wagon showed what happened. We knew the story to be true because occasionally we could find old pieces of wood floating on the surface, which came from the rotting wagon that was resting on the bottom of the deep sinkhole with Ole Man Lawton still on board. In addition to the mystery of Ole Man Lawton, the sinkhole was so deep that once in a while it was a super scary, dark-black color rather than the beautiful blue, which was more common.

We had a rope swing tied to a gigantic tree that hung over the sinkhole, and it was a lot of fun to swing out and drop into the cool water. But before we could safely swim, there was one problem we needed to overcome, which was that snakes and alligators also liked to use Lawton Hole as their hangout. We all knew that one of us had to be the first to jump into the water and chase the snakes and alligators away, but nobody truly wanted to do it. It is difficult to believe, but we actually hoped we could make the moccasins and gators go away by splashing and making a racket. We were afraid but not too scared to let it stop us from using Lawton Hole for our swimming and swinging fun. So every trip to Lawton Hole was accompanied by an argument about who would jump in first. We usually drew straws, but sometimes we just teamed up on someone and teased them until they jumped in screaming and praying.

This was also where I was taught to swim. My father and uncle would tie a rope around our waists and throw us into the sinkhole. If we did not swim as they wished, they would let us sink for a while and then pull us up for a breath and yell "sink or swim" over and over. I am not recommending this technique as the best method for teaching a child to swim, but it did teach me to swim at a young age.

# Chapter Twelve

"Can we ride the horses to the barn?" We asked Uncle Oliver and Daddy if we could ride the horses for the two miles from the unloading area to the horse pen next to the barn.

Jerry Morgan (a cousin) and I were helping unload the horses by the old homestead on an unusually chilly night after bringing them home in a two-horse trailer from the hunting camp. Our families had deer hunted with the horses in Gulf Hammock for the last two weeks, and we were going to be back at the farm for a while, so we brought the horses back home.

Lady and Blaze were both large powerful horses with quarter-horse bloodlines, and they were young and frisky animals. A horse knows when it is heading home to the barn, and it expects food and drink upon arrival. You need to be extremely careful when riding a young horse, or it can get out of control on the way back to the barn.

It was late at night, and the adults were glad we wanted to ride the horses to the barn because they were tired, and it was uncommonly cold. So with their approval, we jumped on the horses and started walking them down the dark-graded road. The adults went ahead in the truck with the horse trailer, and we were alone on the road.

We knew we should not run the horses, but it was not long before we decided to race. I was riding Blaze, and Jerry was riding Lady. Although Lady was much easier to manage, everyone thought she was faster than Blaze. I wanted to prove Blaze could truly outrun Lady. So we started the race about a mile from the barn. It was an even race for a while, and it did not seem to us like either horse could outrun the other, so we decided to stop the race before our parents saw the running horses. Jerry was able to stop Lady, but I was not able to stop Blaze; she was truly a runaway horse headed for the barn. I pulled as hard as I could pull against the reins, but Blaze had the bit in her teeth, and I could not put enough pressure on her mouth to make her stop.

I pulled so hard I broke the left rein, and it popped and flew out of my hand. I could not turn her to the right nor make her stop with one rein. So I just tried to hold on as she raced down the dark road with the freezing wind in my face. Blaze and I passed the truck with Uncle Oliver and Daddy, and I knew they would be angry that we were running the horses. Jerry lagged far behind me, trotting Lady so that he would not get in trouble.

There was a four-foot high fence in the field in front of the barn, which Blaze cleared at full speed; however, there was a taller barbed wire fence next to the barn. When Blaze got close to the barn door and the tall fence, she decided to stop on a dime, and I went flying through the air into the barbed wire. When the adults arrived, Blaze was covered in white sweat against her black body and breathing very hard. I was stuck in the fence with my left eye bleeding like crazy from a barbed spike. As it turns out, it was only my eyelid sliced open. That was my last wild midnight ride, although I still love to ride horses.

# Chapter Thirteen

"Don't swallow the juice," I told Robbie, my brother, that he should spit out the tobacco juice we were chewing, not eat it. Almost all the workers on the farm chewed tobacco, and they made it look pretty cool.

Our father did not use chewing tobacco, but he smoked cigarettes like a house on fire. In fact, he died of lung cancer. Our mother thought it was disgusting to see someone with chewing tobacco and to see one spitting on the ground or in a bottle when they were in the house.

So when my brother and I decided to see what it was like to chew tobacco, we knew we needed to do it in secret. We went to the general store and told the owner we needed some Red Man chewing tobacco for Ernest, one of the hired farmhands. It came in a nice pouch, which we had seen them reach into to get a mouth-sized piece to chew. So we went out to our cardboard fort in the backyard and took out a piece for each of us.

Red Man is exceptionally strong, and it did not taste pleasant, but we tried to keep chewing and spitting just like the guys who use it every day. I managed not to swallow any of the juice. However, Robbie, who is five years younger than me, was not so lucky, and he must have swallowed quite a bit of tobacco juice. We honestly did not like the entire experience, and we decided this had been a terrible idea. We spit out the chew in our mouth and buried all the remaining tobacco behind our little fort after only two minutes of experimenting with Red Man.

All of a sudden, Robbie turned as green as a leaf of lettuce and started puking. It would not have been so awful if our mother had not arrived at exactly that moment and quickly took matters into her capable hands. Robbie told Mother I made him chew the tobacco and that it was my entire fault that he was sick. Maybe he was right, but that is not how I remember the story.

# Chapter Fourteen

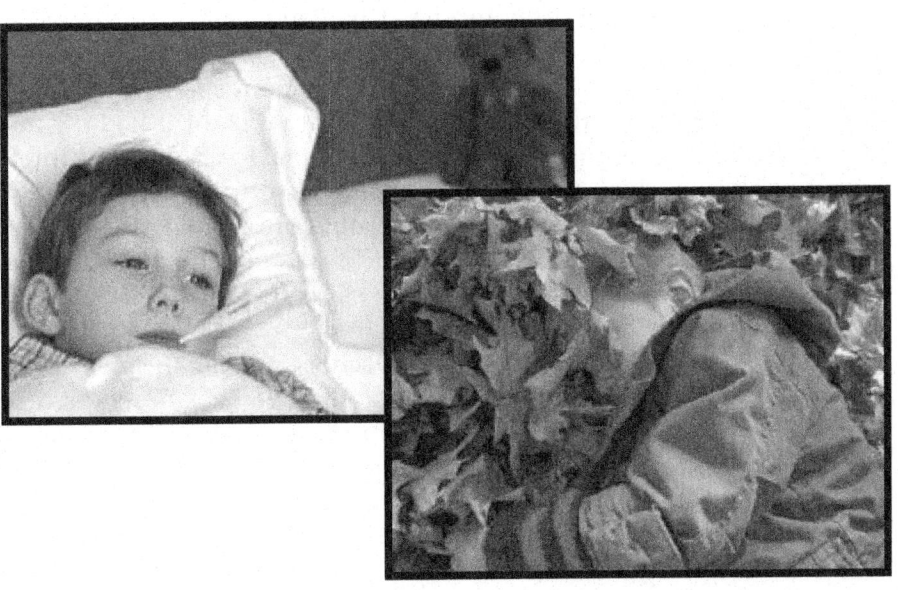

"Stop complaining and rake the leaves." It was November and my mother was exasperated that the huge piles of leaves in our yard were not raked as I had promised.

My right side was hurting, and I did not want to keep raking. She thought I was just faking it to avoid work, but I felt as if something was extremely unusual; nonetheless, I kept on raking. After about one more hour, I told her that I just could not keep working because the pain was getting worse.

So she took me over to one of the neighborhood houses to see Mrs. Radacky, who was a nurse. Mrs. Radacky asked me to explain where I had a pain, and I showed her my right side. She asked me to lie down, and she gently pressed my side, and man o' man did I jump and yell with pain. She told my mother I probably had a busted appendix and that I should go to a hospital. The nearest hospital was in Ocala, twenty-five miles away, and Mother needed to find Daddy who had the only car. After a painful ride, we finally got to the hospital, and they took me right in and almost immediately did an appendectomy.

When I woke up, I heard the strangest voice and words: "Ma, the cows, the cows. They are so big. I cannot find them" and then silence. The man next to me had just died after speaking those words, which I have never forgotten. It was the first time I had ever seen a dead person before they came to take him away. It scared me to know that you can die in the hospital.

The next day, the doctor came to see me and told Mother that something was wrong with my insides. I had spots all over the inside of my body, which he had never seen before and did not know what to do. I was thirteen and was not overly worried about spots in my body, and besides, the cut to my stomach was hurting so badly it had my full attention. After two more days, they sent me home. I was home for three more days during which time cousin Butch tried everything possible to make me laugh so hard that my incision would hurt. Then, just as I was getting better from the appendectomy, I broke out with a world-class case of chicken pox. I guess chicken pox starts on the inside before it appears on the skin.

In those days, you could not return to school until all the scabs were healed and no longer visible. I was so anxious to go back to school that in the next ten days, I scratched off some scabs that left me scarred forever. Just last year, I needed a shingles shot to avoid another case of the chicken pox. Now I think the spots are finally gone.

# Chapter Fifteen

"Grandpa, are those mules good ones?" My grandfather, Buddy Gerald, was a mule trader. He and his family lived in the Ocala area for most of their lives after coming to Florida from South Carolina. He was my mother's father, and he and Granny Gerald had four daughters, all of whom lived just around the corner from each other. Granny Gerald was a well-known home sewer for the wealthy patrons in Ocala. The Geralds were a religious group of Methodists with a strong work ethic and a solid reputation in the community.

Mules, at one time, were an essential part of the farming scene in the rural south and were a prized possession by many farmers and ranchers. As tractors and other farm automation increased, the demand for mules diminished. My grandpa turned to watermelon farming as an alternative way to earn a living. However, he never lost his love for mules and was always on the lookout for the ones that were still around, kept mainly for tradition by a number of farmers.

Looking for watermelon fields to buy, Grandpa would sometimes take me on his trips around the countryside. Grandpa Gerald never planted the melons himself, but he would find a field that he thought looked promising and buy the melons, still on the vine, from the melon farmer. He would then contract to have them picked and delivered to a produce dealer or to a travelling produce buyer for one of the supermarket chains. We almost never made a trip for melons without stopping to look at some mules along the way. Everyone knew Grandpa, and the conversation about the mules and the state of farming was a real learning experience for a young boy.

In case you do not know, a mule is the offspring of a male donkey and a female horse. Mules are infertile, and the size of the mule is primarily dependent upon the size of the female horse. Almost all mule lovers will tell you that mules are more patient, sure-footed, hardy (sort of like Grandpa Gerald), and longer-lived than horses.

My mother nicknamed me Buddy and was extremely proud that I was a lot like my Grandpa "Buddy" Gerald. Even though her father was a mule trader and watermelon agent, she always felt her side of the family was more refined than the Brooks side, and maybe she was correct in some ways. I think the Methodists have always felt superior to the Baptists, but I am not sure.

# Chapter Sixteen

"Don't break open any more melons." I had a nifty little business from age 14 to 17 of hauling watermelons from the farmers' fields to the railroad cars or to the buyers' trucks that were waiting for the melons.

The watermelons were usually ready to harvest in July and August when school was out. My father had an old two-ton truck he used for various things at the farm—trucking to the produce shed, spreading fertilizer, and other tasks. When I got my restricted driver's license at age 14, the law permitted me to drive a vehicle as long as I had a passenger who was eighteen or older in the vehicle with me.

In the summer, I would visit the local watermelon fields as I had learned from my Grandpa Gerald. I would ask the farmers if they needed help hauling the melons from their fields to the location where the buyer had arranged for delivery. We would negotiate the price, which was usually five cents per melon, to pick them up and unload them at the railroad siding or onto another larger truck. On a good day, I could make six loads of around three hundred melons each or a total of $90 for the day.

I needed four men to help me get the melons from the ground into the bed of the truck and then to help unload them at our delivery destination. It was necessary to put the truck into the field where the melons were grown and then move the truck along heap rows lined with melons that had been cut from the vine by the farmer's workhands.

It required two men on either side of the truck and two men on the ground, who would toss the melons from the ground to a man on each side of the inside of the truck. I would pay each of the men $1.50 per load or a total cost of $6.00 per load or $36.00 for the labor for the day. After the cost of gas, I could make almost $40 per day, which was a darned good profit in those days. If I personally stacked the melons into the railroad car or the big truck, I would get another one cent per melon or $18 more for the day. This was an enormous amount of money for a fourteen-year-old to be earning.

Each morning, mainly during July and August, I would drive to an area where a number of black men that wanted work would be waiting. After finding four men—one of whom had to be eighteen—we would head to the field and start working.

One day, I had a significant problem with a young man working on the ground and throwing the melons to another man in the truck, who was catching them and placing them in the straw on the floor of the truck bed. The man on the ground kept breaking open and destroying melons by hitting them on the side of the truck. It was hot in the field, and I felt he was doing it on purpose so that he could take out the heart of the melon and eat it and use the juice to quench his thirst. This was a problem for me because the owner of the field would charge me $1 for every busted melon and subtract it from my pay.

At least five times, I asked him to stop breaking the melons, and he would not listen. We had plenty of cold water on the truck, and he could drink all he needed. So I asked the worker who had been catching the melons to drive, and I would take his place in the bed of the truck. The man on the ground that had been busting the melons was now throwing the melons to me. I could see clearly if he threw the melons against the side of the truck with a purpose. I caught a few melons he tossed as he was expected to do and then he tossed another melon against the truck and broke it open. I decided that he was just being a wise guy, and the next time he broke open a melon, I took one from the bed of the truck and tried to bust it on his head.

He did not like this, and he came after me with a knife. I jumped out of the truck and started running away from him. At one point, he made a swing with the knife and cut my back seriously, but I immediately sped up and was able to make enough headway to grab a stout limb from the ground, turn around, and hit him with it. This stopped him long enough for the owner of the melon field to arrive and take him away.

I learned early. It is not a smart idea to get aggressive with employees.

# Chapter Seventeen

"Butch, I think I hear Raw Head and Bloody Bones outside in the backyard." We did not know about Bigfoot, Sasquatch, Yeti, the Loch Ness Monster, or the Hounds of the Baskervilles, but we had our own scary bogeyman called Raw Head and Bloody Bones!

I have recently done some research, and John Locke first mentioned this creature in 1693 to "awe children and keep them in subjection." There were also stories from the African Americans living on the farm that included Raw Headed and Bloody Bones. Since we had an English—and Scottish-mixed heritage and blacks living on the farm, this story found its way to our family as a legend.

According to some definitions, Bloody Bones is said to live near ponds, but according to Ruth Tongue in *Somerset Folklore,* he "lived in a dark cupboard, usually under the stairs. If you were heroic enough to peep, through a crack, you would get a glimpse of the dreadful, crouching creature, with blood running down his face, seated waiting on a pile of raw bones that had belonged to children who told lies or said bad words." We had no stairs in our house, but we did have a pond in the field behind the house.

If we did things not to the liking of our fathers, they warned us about the presence and possible action of Bloody Bones. Whatever contemporary comments there are about this guy, our blood would grow cold at the mention of him being in our yard.

There were propane gas tanks outside the window to my bedroom when we still lived at the farm, and they made a ringing sound if hit by some object. If warned about a Bloody Bones sighting, I stayed awake listening for the propane tanks to make a noise as a signal that he was climbing into my room. Then I could run as fast as possible to my parents' bedroom for safety.

Butch would often sleepover, and the two of us took considerable comfort in sharing our fright with one another. I never saw Bloody Bones, but he sure was real enough to scare me.

# Chapter Eighteen

"Jerry, run! Look out for the snake." The biggest and meanest snake I ever saw before going to a zoo was a rusty stump-tail moccasin that Jerry Morgan and I encountered at Sandy Bottom. I know that many of you will think it was just a large Florida cottonmouth, but I am sure it was the legendary rusty stump-tail moccasin.

Jerry and I had driven one of the tractors to Sandy Bottom, a tranquil and beautiful section of water adjacent to the big lake to fish for bass. We were plugging with Dalton Specials, which look like frogs and are exceptionally suitable for catching monster bass. After a beautiful long cast, I had my plug just about back along the water's edge when a sizable commotion occurred right in front of Jerry and me. First, I thought it was a fish, but very quickly, I saw it was a giant snake that had mistaken the plug for a real frog.

The snake was not hooked, but it rose up on its tail, opened its large white mouth, and struck at the plug several times. I had never seen a snake stand up before and could not believe my eyes. Jerry and I decided to run like the devil for the tractor, and I think we threw our fishing rods into the lake as we ran away.

Well, unbelievably, the snake came after us hissing and striking. This snake was over six feet long with a diameter of at least six inches, and its behavior made it the most aggressive snake you can imagine. To get above the snake who was striking wildly, we jumped on the hood of the tractor. When the snake finally stopped striking and started moving away, we quickly got down to the seat of the tractor, cranked it up, and decided to drive over the darn thing and kill it.

Well, it was no easy task to avoid the angry strikes and still run over the snake without getting bitten ourselves. We almost ran over a hog or two in our efforts to kill the snake. The hogs, which were often in that area, were foraging for acorns and other food in the woods near Sandy Bottom.

Despite our fear, we did manage to run over the snake many times before we were confident it was dead. We were afraid to pick it up, and so we left it there. When we told everyone about killing the big snake, of course, they wanted to see it. We all returned to Sandy Bottom, but the snake was gone. To this day, not everyone believes our story, but I can tell you for sure it is true. I think one of the hogs must have taken the snake and eaten it as they will do to supplement their diet.

# Chapter Nineteen

$$\frac{2}{3} \div \frac{4}{5} = \frac{2}{3} \times \frac{5}{4}$$
$$= \frac{2 \times 5}{3 \times 4}$$
$$= \frac{10}{12}$$
$$= \frac{5}{6}$$

"I do not understand how to divide fractions." My cousin, Baker, was the smartest guy in our class at school. Baker is only nine months older than I am, and we were in the same class from the first grade through graduation from high school.

Baker was adept at math, and he always seemed to get the idea of new math concepts a few days before me. We would study together sometimes at Mema and Grandpa's house where Baker, Butch, and Nanada were living after Uncle Oliver and Aunt Mildred separated. Grandpa Brooks was also skilled at math, and he and Baker could certainly surprise all of us with their knowledge of fractions and other more complicated stuff as we all learned algebra and geometry.

Mr. Maynard was our math teacher at school, and he used Baker and Naomi, a lovely classmate, as examples of the math leaders in our classes for years. I always felt happy knowing that Baker was there to help with a math problem, and I got pretty proficient at math myself as time progressed.

Later, when Baker and I entered the University of Florida, we were both assigned the honors' math classes based on our test scores. The math classes were tougher for me than they were for Baker. I started with a major in engineering at UF but later shifted my studies to accounting at Jacksonville University.

I have always been good with numbers but not necessarily complicated mathematics. Oh well, one cannot be expert at everything, can they?

# Chapter Twenty

"Jo Ann is the new Rodeo Queen!" My sister, Jo Ann, was elected Rodeo Queen in 1950 when she was a senior in high school. I remember her riding in the parade wearing a leather crown, and our entire family was so proud of her selection.

I was still young (ten years old), and to have my sister as queen of the parade was a significant event. We had that crown for years, and recently, I have been wondering what happened to it. The local ranchers, farmers, and horse owners loved to show their skills and animals at the annual rodeo. It was an unusually festive occasion when the rodeo was in town. People would also come from the nearby towns, and the crowds would be surprisingly large and enthusiastic, bringing their horses and other animals to show.

Jo Ann was also smart; in fact, she was valedictorian of her class just like Daddy had been years before. Jo Ann gave me a copy of Daddy's valedictory speech a few years back. His speech was truly filled with glorious dreams that, unfortunately, never happened for him. I was particularly moved by the following paragraph in his valedictorian speech, which was given in 1928: "We realize that our lives up to this present time have been practically untroubled, and our sailing has been over tranquil waters. We know that when we have left this past our voyage will be over the rough and rugged sea of life—yet we do not shrink from what we see before us but go forward with heads held high and the light of battle in our eyes." While his destiny was not as he envisioned, he did have time to see many of his dreams come true for his children and grandchildren.

Among many community events, the rodeo was just one in which our family participated. While poor, we were involved in most local activities, and we felt we were an integral part of our community. All of us—siblings and our children and grandchildren—have continued to be involved in community affairs wherever we have lived.

# Chapter Twenty-One

"Honeypie, let's go to the movies with Robbie." My sister Sara (Honeypie), my brother, Robbie, and I begged to see the new movie playing in our town called *The Thing*. We lived in a small rental house about five blocks from the only movie theater in Williston.

Robbie is five years younger than me, and Sara is seven years younger. Mother gave us enough money to pay for the movie, some popcorn, and a Coke each. I remember that we got our seats and were so excited to watch the movie we could hardly wait. As was customary in those days, first we had to watch a cartoon or two, then a cowboy serial (*Hopalong Cassidy*, I think) and then the movie.

*The Thing* is a totally scary movie where a plant can take different forms, and it is especially scary for kids as young as we were. We left the movie wondering if there could actually be evil plantlike creatures on this planet.

Along the route from the movie to our house were large oak trees filled with Spanish moss that eerily move with the wind, and during the day, they are beautiful, but at night, they can look like ghosts. It was with this background of a scary movie and a scary walk home, which caused me to run ahead of Sara and Robbie and leave them behind. They were young and afraid to be alone in the dark.

Once out of sight, I hid behind a towering oak tree near the path home, covered myself with some moss, and when they just got past the tree, I jumped out and yelled and growled. They both jumped at least three feet into the air and screamed. I thought it was extremely funny, but they did not share my point of view, and I paid for it when we got home.

Whatever the reason, I have always liked to scare people as a joke, and it gives me a belly laugh when they jump and look startled.

# Chapter Twenty-Two

"Big Boy, we need more peat moss to the conveyor bin right now!" To help make the money we needed to live, my mother, Rubye, worked at many jobs in her lifetime. One of her jobs in the summer was to supervise a group of about twenty women at JP Sandlin's tomato plant shed.

In the 1950s, tomato farmers did not usually raise their own tomato plants but, rather, bought them from certified specialists who raised the plants to a height of about ten to twelve inches. The plants were removed from the soil, and the roots of the plants needed to be quickly wrapped in a peat moss and water mixture to prepare them for shipment to the actual tomato farmers.

This process would keep the plants alive until they were received and transplanted by the actual tomato farmer in Tennessee or some other state farther north. Mr. Sandlin had a long-standing business of growing plants. To prepare the plants for shipping north, he rented the old railroad platform and set up a conveyor belt contraption to move the plants along a row of women who would wrap the plants in the peat moss mixture and secure them with a brown paper wrapper. He would buy the peat moss from folks who lived in the Everglades area near Orlando, and the peat moss was trucked to the railroad shed. There was a large area where the dry peat moss was dumped on the ground near the platform.

Every year, mother hired Big Boy, a large African American, and me to mix the dry peat moss with water then put the mixture in a wheelbarrow, push the wheelbarrow up a long ramp to the conveyor bin, shovel the wet mixture into boxes adjacent to the women working on the conveyor belt, and keep the women furnished with the wet mixture as another worker laid the plants on the belt.

Now folks, this was heavy hard work! Keeping up with the demand for peat moss was almost as frustrating as Sisyphus pushing his rock up the mountain. Big Boy and I could not keep the conveyor belt full of wet peat moss without the most constant diligent and speedy work. Mother and the women were always yelling that they needed wet peat moss, and they needed it immediately. Twelve hours a day of pushing the two wheelbarrows up the ramp and unloading them into the wet bin is the hardest work I ever had to do. Over the years, Big Boy developed an enormous hernia that was bigger than two grapefruits, which was obvious to the eye even through his baggy coveralls. I saw him a few years ago, and he still had the hernia because he could not afford to have it repaired. As for me, I have had three hernias repaired in my groin area, and I guess maybe the peat moss work gave them to both Big Boy and me.

# Chapter Twenty-Three

"Hey, peanut boy, bring us some boiled peanuts." Many farmers in our region raised peanuts for a living. In those days, a peanut allotment, provided by the government, was a precious thing to have.

    A farmer could produce all the peanuts he needed for animal feed, but not for sale commercially without an allotment. An allotment meant the government would guarantee a certain price for all the peanuts raised on a specific number of acres. The Fugates had the largest allotments followed by a few other families. Uncle Oliver had a relatively small allotment, and Uncle Burke had a large allotment, but my father had lost his allotment when he lost the farm. In any event, peanuts were a popular crop, and they were eaten by our community in a variety of ways; they were eaten raw, roasted, salted, and boiled. Most people around the world do not eat them boiled, but in our area, it was the preferred taste.

The raw green peanuts were placed in a pressure cooker with a perfect amount of salt and left to boil for just the right amount of time, which was a family secret. When the process was over, the feast would begin, and we could eat tons of peanuts. Once you started eating them, it was like eating potato chips, you could hardly stop. We would make them in large quantities and freeze what we could not eat right away. They were better fresh but still mighty tasty even if they had been frozen.

Throughout the year, on many Saturdays, my mother would make boiled peanuts and put them in small paper bags, which she would place in a shallow cardboard box or a basket that could carry about twenty bags. She would give the cardboard box loaded with bags for me to sell on the streets of our little town for a dime per bag. When I sold all the bags in one box or basket, she would fill me up again and send me back out to sell more.

Most of the time, I would stand on the corner where the townsmen and community leaders would meet and hope they would buy some peanuts. Sometimes, I would walk the streets saying, "Boiled peanuts, one dime!" A few years later, when the city gave me a scholarship to go to college, they made a point of calling me the "peanut boy" because that is how most people in town knew me.

I think I was invisible to the men because they did not pay me any attention unless they wanted a bag of peanuts, and they did not stop their conversations when I was around. As a result, I overheard and learned many things about our town and their "ideas" about business, politics, and women. These were mostly subjects not discussed during the church services where they were often the deacons and elders.

I was surprised, puzzled, shocked, and intrigued by the contrast in behavior between the street and the church. When I was the youth week minister at the First Baptist Church, I made my sermons on the twenty-third chapter of Matthew. They were sermons about the perils of hypocrisy.

I learned a lot about human nature and how to sell as a peanut boy.

# Chapter Twenty-Four

"What can that scratching be?" I was turkey hunting in Gulf Hammock, deep in the woods, near Ten Mile Creek.

I had hidden in the middle of a clump of roots and weeds, created from a tree that had been blown over by a recent hurricane. The hole made in the soil, where the roots had once been growing, was overgrown with green weeds, and it provided an excellent blind in front of me. The upended roots and the long tree trunk, which extended far behind me, provided the perfect spot to conceal my presence from the rear.

So I was exceptionally well hidden, and I hoped to use a turkey call that sounded like a female turkey to entice some male turkeys to come visiting. My father had made a turkey call with a combination of a piece of slate and a corncob with a piece of cedar in the middle. I would rub the cedar rod against the slate, and it made a sound like a turkey. The key was to be extremely still, make no movement that could be seen by the keen-eyed turkeys, and make a realistic-sounding call.

I was doing everything right, and I heard some turkeys in the distance coming toward me. The swamp was thick with trees, bushes, and vines, and I could not see more than fifty yards in front of me. The turkeys in the distance would answer my call only occasionally, so I could not tell how far away they were, but I was getting excited and increasingly confident that I was going home with a prized gobbler (male turkey).

Then I heard a scratching noise close behind me. I thought maybe that it was a turkey walking along the tree trunk. Then I thought that was silly and maybe it was just the wind. The scratching got a little louder, and soon it was darned close; maybe no more than ten feet behind me.

I decide to whirl around and point my gun in the direction of the noise, and I expected to see a turkey, but instead, I saw a bobcat with its mouth wide open. The bobcat thought I was a turkey, and I thought he was a turkey; we both surprised each other. Thankfully, he jumped sky-high and ran away, and I involuntarily dropped my gun, startled beyond belief. I sat down and tried to fathom what had just happened, thinking how close I had come to being the dinner of a bobcat.

I quickly decided turkey hunting was no longer any fun when the hunter becomes the hunted. Since that day, I have done no more turkey hunting in the woods.

# Chapter Twenty-Five

"Man, that is a big fire!" It was unusually cold, but Butch and I were told to take the toilet paper trail back into the woods near the old tram and wait for the dogs to chase a deer our way.

A few days before, some of our parents had made a trail deep into the woods using toilet papers to hang from the bushes. It was perhaps a bright idea for a fairy tale, but it did not work so well in Gulf Hammock. It had been raining constantly for days, and the rain and the wind had destroyed the trail, which was intended to show us the way to the old tram road. We quickly got lost and encountered a large pond blocking our way. We debated what to do but finally decided we would get in trouble if we were not in place when the dogs ran a deer our way. So we waded through the pond and got soaking wet.

When we got to the location in the woods that we felt was about where they wanted us to be, we were so cold that our bodies were shaking like leaves in the wind. We decided we needed to build a fire, dry our clothes, and warm up. We started the fire, took off our clothes, and stood naked as close to the fire for warmth as possible. We heard the dogs coming our way.

I know you will not believe it, but the dogs ran a bunch of wild hogs right through the fire. We did not have our guns in our hands, and we ran to avoid the hogs getting us. We got a little lost, and when we came back to what had been a small fire, it was now an enormous, out-of-control inferno. We did not know how to contain the fire, so we cut the top from some small pine trees and used them in an attempt to stamp out the fire. This approach did not work well at all, and the fire grew and grew in size.

We stopped to put on our wet clothes. Then we just kept trying to beat the fire with the treetops in hopes we could stop it. When the adults found the fire and us, we were black from the flames and scared to death. It took quite a while for everyone, including a group of game wardens, to put out the fire that eventually burned around forty acres.

There have been a few times in my adult life that I have remembered this experience and felt as if I was trying to put out a roaring fire with a treetop.

# Chapter Twenty-Six

"What is that on my face?" The night was clear, the moon was full, and the sky was filled with countless stars that seemed to be just a mile away.

We were riding the horses on the prairie around Stafford Pond at a period of time when the water was unusually low, and the dry ground made the area perfect for a foxhunt. There were thousands of acres on which we could ride and hunt and almost no fences. We had a few hounds with us, some blue ticks, redbones, and beagles. There was me, Jerry Morgan, and Butch Brooks. We were in no hurry, and the dogs were not either. It was a perfect time to be together with no cares, no problems, and no rush.

We had just eaten a couple of sandwiches when one of the beagles struck a fresh fox scent and started the chase. The dogs were out in front of us, and we were galloping along at a nice but unhurried pace. The dogs had not yet actually seen the fox, and so the chase was not as heated as it would get. We came upon a low area that contained some water. I thought the water would only be a foot or too deep and decided to gallop the horse through the water splashing and laughing. It was not shallow, and the horse and I got soaked and almost bogged down in the soft mud.

The pond was covered with green mossy scum of some kind, and I thought there might be moccasins in the water. I quickly turned the horse to the left near a large oak tree since I thought the water level near the tree would be shallower. As we got near the tree, I felt something cling to my face.

Without any thought, I slapped at the thing on my face then something popped. I immediately felt thousands of small things on my face, so I started slapping, scrapping, and thinking to try to understand what had happened. I suddenly realized that I had run into a spiderweb hanging from the tree occupied by an enormous wolf spider carrying a huge egg filled with thousands of tiny spiders. When I slapped my face, I popped the egg, and the baby spiders were crawling all over me. I had only one thought: get them off my face and body. So despite the green scum and fear of snakes, I jumped into the pond and frantically washed the spiders from my face and body. I took off all of my clothes and rode naked for an hour while we finished the foxhunt, looking constantly for more spiders. I cannot remember the details of the fox we finally treed, but I do remember the spiders, and I hate spiders to this day!

# Chapter Twenty-Seven

"Son, I will show you how to collect the money you are owed." Daddy woke me up one night around 11:00 p.m. and said we were going to collect the money that Frog owed us.

I had made a deal with a guy named Frog to carry his watermelons from a field he had bought to the railroad terminal. He was almost a stranger, but we had seen him around town a few times, and he drove a beautiful new Lincoln convertible car. I was young and had always worked for local farmers who I knew, so I trusted Frog.

I worked a week for him, taking many loads of melons to the railroad, and he owed me around $500, which was a lot of money. I had paid for gas and for the labor out of my own pocket. After we had loaded the last of the melons onto the railcar, I asked Frog for my money. Frog said he needed to go to the bank to get the money, and he would pay me tomorrow. I said OK. I never saw Frog again, and it had been about six months since he left town without paying me. My father had been angry at me for being so foolish, but he had been unusually angry at Frog for taking advantage of me.

That night, I got in the truck with my father, who had consumed only a few drinks, and we drove to a bar on the north side of town known to be a rough place. My father carried his twelve-gauge shotgun, which he kept in his truck with him as we walked into the bar.

Frog was sitting at the bar having a drink, and without any words, my father put the shotgun into Frog's mouth. He asked Frog if he had $500 in cash with him. Frog shook his head no. My father asked him if he had his checkbook in his pocket. He nodded yes. My father asked him to write me a check while the gun barrel was still in his mouth.

Frog wrote the check. My father suggested that he not let the check bounce. We left the bar without another word. The check did not bounce, and Frog did not come back to do any more watermelon business in our town.

I realized that technique is not the recommended approach for collecting most bills today, and it is not a method I suggest any of you follow.

# Chapter Twenty-Eight

Marvin Prince

Alan Brooks

Bobby Sandlin

FIRST ROW, Left to Right: John Hopping, Jeff Andrews, Burke Brooks, Noah Long, Carroll Sandlin. SECOND ROW: George Wynn, Johnny Tyner, Harold Griffin, Woodrow Folsom. THIRD ROW: Ernest Blitch, Robert Stanley, Harry Bradford.

Page Seventy-Three

"Alan, go to the dressing room. You are out of the game." There were exceedingly few cultural events in our town, and high school sports were one of the most popular activities our community enjoyed almost all year long.

Our football, basketball, and baseball games were well attended by the local townsfolk. I played football and basketball, but baseball season was, at a time of the year, that conflicted with the harvest of our watermelons, squash, cucumbers, and other fresh vegetables.

I started playing football in the eighth grade at the position of right end. I was a decent player and was recommended as an all-conference player in the tenth grade. When I was in the eleventh grade, the principal called a meeting in the cafeteria with the coach, some parents, and our team to talk about our prospects for a winning season. This was a bit unusual, but everyone thought we had an excellent chance to be the conference champions. To my surprise, the principal (not the coach) asked me to stand up, and he praised my skills as a right end. Then he asked me to give up my chance to be all-conference and made a personal appeal for me to play the position of left guard, which was a spot we needed to fill to win, and reluctantly, I agreed.

Well, we practiced and practiced, and I learned my new position well. On our team, if you played both offense and defense and if you were a left guard, you played the same position on both. Our first opponent was Cross City, who had the reputation for being the toughest, roughest, and meanest team in our conference. I was a little worried because the guy who would play against me was a senior who had been all-conference twice. As we lined up for the first play, he took off his helmet. He showed me that he had only one ear and told me that by the end of the game, I too would only have one ear since he was planning to bite off one of mine. This made my decision to play guard, rather than to stay at the end position, seem like a poor choice. Well, I played hard, and I kept both of my ears, and we ultimately won the game. However, as you can see from this story, I do still remember that game and one tough kid from Cross City.

I also played basketball and was the sixth man on a five-man team. That meant I got to play when Bobby Sandlin was tired or not performing well. In my senior year, we made it to the conference semifinals, and my father decided to come to the game that was an away game in Chiefland.

My father did not attend many games, and he had not seen me play that much. We were now in the third quarter; I had only been in the game a few times for less than a total of five minutes, and I had only scored two points. Bobby was not playing very well, and my father thought I should be put in the game. He came down to the bench and gave his opinion to the coach very loudly. The coach immediately said, "Alan, go to the dressing room. You are out of the game." He would not tolerate any comments or opinions from any parents, and he wanted to prove how strongly he felt about parental interference. I was hugely disappointed not to play anymore in that game. We did win the game, and I got to play some more in the finals.

Even today, I agree with the decision of Coach Durrance, and I think parents should not get involved with the coaches' decisions.

# Chapter Twenty-Nine

"Ms. Amelia, can I have a Moon Pie?" Ms. Amelia and Ms. Agnes ran a small general store in Montbrook.

Ms. Amelia was the postmaster for the area; their little store had the mail, milk, bread, some canned goods, flour, sodas, candy, and some cakes called Moon Pies. I truly loved a Strawberry soda and a moon pie, and I still enjoy that childhood delight.

Ms. Amelia inherited her small property from her father who had been a Union soldier in the Civil War. Somewhat surprisingly, some Union soldiers were given land in the southern states after the war. All of us could walk down to the store at any time because it was just a short distance from our homes. We just needed someone to give us twenty-five cents, and we could get a soda and a cake.

Enormous sprawling oak trees grew in the area next to the store with some old benches under them, and we would get our sodas and cakes and eat them under the trees. We had lots to talk about and stories to tell under those massive oaks, who had listened to numerous tall tales over many years.

Directly across the street from the store was an old rundown building that had once been a saloon, and it contained an actual piece of a bloody history about our family. Great-grandpa Montholon was pistol-whipped by a cousin in that saloon. His son, my Grandpa Brooks, felt that he must defend the family honor, and when he heard of the beating and saw the damage to his father, he immediately travelled by horse to Cousin Will's house, called him out, and shot him dead.

This caused a family feud, and my father and Uncle Oliver hid under their house and shot it out with the cousins when they came to avenge the killing. Grandpa Brooks did go to jail for a while, and the legend of the Brooks killing and the subsequent events remain to this day.

Honor is essential to maintain, but it often needs restraint.

# Chapter Thirty

"Grandpa, how can you eat squirrel brains?" We hunted and ate many things that were around the farm and in Gulf Hammock, which was a designated Florida State hunting preserve around twenty miles away.

We hunted for deer, turkey, dove, quail, duck, squirrel, wild hog, and occasionally, bear. We also raised cattle, hogs, sometimes goats, chickens, guinea hens (who had eggs as hard as rocks), and turkeys. Between the game and domestic animals, a large part of the meat we consumed was killed, cleaned, preserved, and cooked by the family. In addition to those items mentioned above, the help living on the farm enjoyed raccoons, and a few would eat possums that were numerous.

The family ate almost every part of every animal: tripe, which is the stomach of cattle; hogshead cheese is made from the brains of hogs;

chitlins are pig intestines; pickled pig's feet; cracklings are pig skin and fat; calf brains; bull testicles; hog testicles (known as mountain oysters); pig snouts; and sausages from hogs, cattle, and deer.

Also on the farm were land turtles that we called gophers that could weigh up to ten pounds. They burrowed holes in the sandy soil that left large white mounds of dirt visible to the eye. The black helpers who lived on the farm loved the taste of these gophers, and we could sell the gophers to them for a few cents if we could capture them.

The primary method used to catch a gopher was to pull them from deep in their hole, which could be ten to fifteen feet deep with a long pole with a hook on it. We would push the pole into the gopher hole, searching for the gopher by feeling, turning the pole repeatedly with a slight pull to catch the hook under the shell of the gopher and then once connected, we would pull like the devil to bring them out of the hole.

There was one significant threat to gopher pulling—rattlesnakes like to share the hole with the gopher, and we needed to be careful to see what we were actually pulling out. More than one time, we pulled out snakes rather than gophers, and although some of the folks would eat snake meat, we did not intentionally hunt for snakes. Occasionally, we would see a gopher crawling around the fields outside of their hole, and we would run quickly to them and carefully pick them up by their shell and put them in the back of our pickup truck—this was the easiest and safest method, but not the most productive.

While it was customary to eat many of the things above, I do believe that Grandpa Brooks was the only person who ate squirrel brains. He would take a boiled squirrel's head and use a heavy spoon to crack the skull and scoop out the brains and eat them. He felt it made him smarter. While Grandpa Brooks was a remarkably intelligent man, I simply do not believe squirrel brains were the reason.

# Chapter Thirty-One

"I love to ride horses and dress up like a cowboy." I always liked to dress up in whatever outfit was in tune with the day and the moment. Many people in our area rode horses all the time—to work, to school, and for fun. I wanted to be like them and like the cowboys we saw at the movies almost every week.

Mother also dressed us up for Halloween, Easter, and for churchgoing. She taught us to dress properly for whatever function was occurring at the moment. I was involved in many school activities, and I loved to be in a football uniform, a basketball outfit, and a band uniform. During the football games, when there was halftime, I would march in the band in my football uniform since I played both on the football team and first trumpet in the band. I was also one of the leads in both our junior and senior plays and thoroughly enjoyed pretending to be someone else for a while.

For students who liked to play many roles (football, basketball, baseball, track, and band), our school was perfect. It was small enough for a person to be involved in almost every activity. We only had around forty students in my graduating class, and Baker and I were actively involved in the school affairs.

I do not remember the reason, but one year, they planted some trees in our honor (along with some other class members) near the goal posts on the south end of the practice football field. I think it was recognition as class officers but maybe for some other school activity. I cannot recall the exact reason, but I still remember the honor.

I think Baker and I have both outlived the trees, and that is a good thing.

In the photo above, my mother had dressed me up to look like one of the stars that were in the movies and series that ran every Saturday. The stars were names like the Lone Ranger, Hopalong Cassidy, Lash Larue, Gene Autry, Roy Rogers, and others.

Today, I still think one should dress the part: look like a businessman when conducting business, a golfer when playing golf, a fisherman when fishing, and a cowboy when riding horses.

# Chapter Thirty-Two

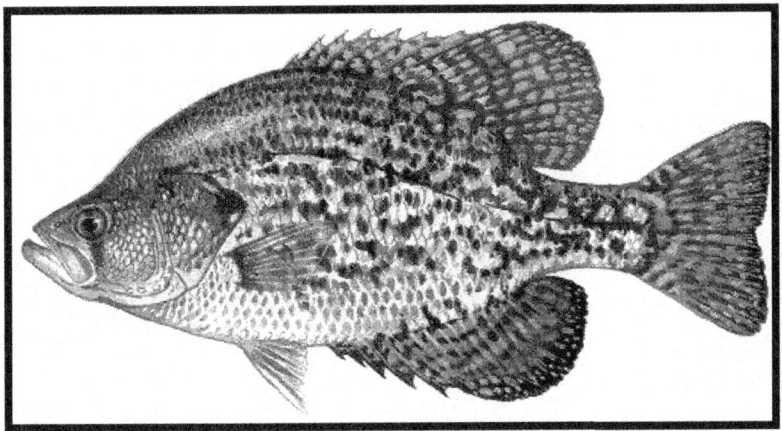

"Wow, how many have we caught?" Mother, Daddy, and I were fishing on Lake George in the Ocala National Forest.

It was in the month of March, and it was so cold you would not believe it. We were in a small rented wooden boat with a ten-horsepower motor, fishing for speckled perch (specs), also known as crappies. Speckled perch are delicious to eat; they taste truly exceptional when fried to a golden brown and served with some grits and cheese. They also fight pretty well for a one—or two-pound fish, and during their spawning season from February to April, they are remarkably active biters.

They will eat a lot of different baits, but the best are the small minnows we had purchased at the fish camp where we rented the boat and motor. Each of us had two cane poles with a cork adjusted to set the bait at a different level in the water as we drifted with the wind across the lake. When we got a bite, we would immediately throw the anchor overboard to stop the boat and fish that area for a while until they stop biting.

During this period, specs tend to nest in colonies, and when you find the right spot, you can load the boat with them. Often we would take home one-hundred fish or more, and it would take Daddy and me a long time to clean all of them. My parents loved spec fishing more than any other type of fishing because of the sheer pleasure it provided and the potential to put a large number of fish in the freezer to enjoy later.

I never heard my mother laugh with more absolute delight than when she had a spec on both poles, and the fish were pulling like the dickens. This is one of my most pleasant memories of being with them when they were both happy and in harmony with each other and me.

# Chapter Thirty-Three

"Get him off of me, help me, and get him off of me." We were playing a game called the fox and the hound.

Butch, Ernest, and I were down near the barn and the horse pens with nothing to do but have some fun. We had been plowing all day, but we were finished, and it was just before dusk. We decided to play the game we call the fox and the hound. The game is almost like hide-and-seek except when you locate the fox, you also need to catch him and tag him and then he becomes the hound, and the game starts over.

Ernest, one of our farmworkers, was the hound. He had to go into the barn where he could not see and give us five minutes to go hide before he could start looking for us. I decided to climb a large bushy tree about one hundred yards from the barn. There was a real sandy area under the tree, and I carefully covered my tracks by dragging a small bush behind me that I took up the tree with me.

About thirty feet up in the tree, I reached up for a limb while looking through the leaves and scanning to see if Ernest was anywhere near. I wanted to move slowly to avoid being seen, and I was not looking directly at the limbs above my head but feeling my way up the tree with my hands. Instead of finding a limb, I put my hand around an enormous pine snake without realizing what was in my hand, and I squeezed hard to pull myself higher. Thank the Lord, a pine snake is not poisonous, but I did not know what I had in my hand, and I assumed the worst.

Well, let me tell you a little about pine snakes as confirmed by Wikipedia. Pine snakes are large, heavy-bodied snakes that average four to six feet long and are powerfully built. The color of pine snakes may be white, yellow, brown, or light gray. The Florida pine snake generally is browner in coloration than the northern pine snakes, which is the reason I thought it was a limb. When disturbed, it will hiss loudly, flatten its head, vibrate its tail, and eventually, strike at an intruder, which was me. I probably do not need to tell you that I immediately forgot about being quiet and unseen by Ernest. All of a sudden, the most important thing was for me to get rid of that snake which had wrapped around my arm and was hissing like crazy. I fell out of the tree, hitting limbs and leaves on the way down, which broke my fall, but it did not release the snake from my arm.

Once on the ground, I started slinging my arm super hard, and somehow, the snake flew off my arm and wrapped itself around Ernest's neck, who had come to help me. Now, the make-believe hound was jumping and hollering and slinging his arms and pulling at the snake until it flew off and hit the ground with a *thud.* The size of Ernest's eyes were about the same size as mature grapefruits, and he was stuttering so much I could not understand a thing he was trying to say, and I was in the same state of terror-induced hysteria.

The real hounds, who hung out in the barnyard area, heard the noise we were making and came over to see what was going on. When they spotted the snake on the ground, the dogs started barking and biting the snake, but eventually, it crawled into the woods and found a hole in which to escape. I have never climbed a tree again without being sure I was going to pull myself up with a limb and not a snake that looked like a limb.

I think this was a strong lesson for me as I tried to pull myself up in the business world; make sure the thing that is helping you climb the ladder of success in a solid thing of value, not a snake.

# Chapter Thirty-Four

"Boy, that BBQ meat smells good." Uncle Oliver had many BBQs at his farmhouse over the years.

There were all manner of relatives, friends, and guests. As many as one hundred people would spend an entire afternoon cooking, talking, storytelling, eating, drinking, and playing music. He had an immense BBQ grill that had been custom-made for him. It was probably fifteen feet long, four feet wide, and four feet high. It was made of steel with a remarkably strong grill screen that could support several hundred pounds of meat and vegetables.

A few days before the BBQ, we would go into the woods and cut down small oak trees and make logs from them. Large quantities of logs were placed under the grilling surface the night before the BBQ was to begin. Once lighted, they would burn all night so that the coals were just perfect in the morning for the BBQ'ing to begin around 10:00 a.m. During the day, it might be necessary to toss a few more logs on the fire to maintain the temperature exactly as desired.

Uncle Oliver and we, little helpers, would go into town the morning of the BBQ to get the meat. Some of the meat would be in the icehouse where the game, killed while hunting, had been stored. Other meats were purchased at the local grocery store.

There would be venison (deer meat), wild hog, farm-raised hog, beef, and maybe some turkey or chicken for those who did not eat meat. If any quail, dove, or squirrels had been recently killed, they would be tossed on the grill as well. He would use a home mixture of various ingredients to make the BBQ sauce, which was applied to the meat constantly throughout the four to six hours of slow cooking. It was a sweet BBQ sauce and might contain tomato sauce, tomato paste, vinegar, brown sugar, olive oil, Worcestershire sauce, paprika, chili powder, onion, garlic, and other spices he felt would give it his unique flavor. Whatever he put in the sauce, most folks agreed he did a superb job of giving the BBQ a fantastic flavor enjoyed by all.

The women would bring all kinds of food to go along with the BBQ. There were mounds of potato salad, roasted corn, coleslaw, grilled vegetables, baked beans, salads, and Jell-O molds plus an array of desserts that included cakes and pies of all descriptions.

Most of the adults drank beer and a lot of it. The beer cans and bottles would be chilled in washtubs or large galvanized buckets placed on the ground and filled with ice. Many of the guests would bring their own beer and toss it into the tubs of ice scattered around the backyard. The radio would be tuned to a country-western station, providing a perfect complement to the laughter and general enjoyment of the crowd. The kids would play all kinds of fun games: hide-and-seek, horseback riding, mumble-the-peg, marbles, shoot BB guns at cans (when older we would use .22 rifles for target contests), wrestling, and lots of eating during the day.

The kids were given the task of making the ice cream. We used a manual churn, which included a cylinder filled with homemade ice cream ingredients and surrounded by ice and ice salt. As the ice cream mixture became firmer, the handle got harder and harder to turn, and we had to take shifts sitting on the top of the churn, giving it weight and improved stability. We got a cold bottom, but it was worth it knowing that we were about to get a real treat.

Uncle Oliver was a popular man, and his BBQs served as a way for him to entertain a large number of his friends and family at the same time.

There are many fancy ways to entertain, but a country BBQ is hard to top even with a cold bottom in the deal.

# Chapter Thirty-Five

"I want two hundred pounds of oranges." In 1956, Mother opened a fruit shop across the street from the Dairy Queen to try to find a way to earn some money.

We rented a little building that also served as our home, and it had a small room facing the street that she used as the fruit shop. The small space was part of the rental payment we made for our living quarters, so it did not cost any extra rent money to create the fruit shop.

There was a sidewalk in front of the building where we placed bags of oranges, grapefruits, peaches (when we could get them), coconuts, and maybe some bags of pecans when they were in season. Inside the shop, we sold fresh orange juice and candies such as, chocolate-covered coconut patties, Mounds, Snickers, Mary Janes, chewing gum, and other popular chocolate delights. We had sodas and a few postcards showing various places in Florida. It was a cute little place but remarkably simple. Our main customers were the tourists who were passing through our town on their way to somewhere else as there was no reason for a tourist to visit Williston.

To keep the shop profitable, it was necessary to buy fresh oranges and grapefruits from a wholesaler in bulk, then bag them and sell them before they got too soft from old age to be appealing to a buyer. When they started getting soft or getting to the point where they did not look firm, we would squeeze them for juice that was downright delicious and sweet. We never sold nor used decayed fruit for juice, so we needed to make sure we bought just the right amount of oranges in bulk from the wholesaler. If we bought too many oranges, we would lose money; and if we did not buy enough oranges, we would lose sales.

At this time, Daddy was not able to help much at all due to his drinking. We had an old green Chevrolet pickup truck that we used as a second vehicle. Mother would send me to Weirsdale to buy the oranges in bulk. It was around forty miles from our shop in the middle of an orange-growing part of Florida, and there were a number of orange wholesalers. Some wholesalers were also fruit growers and often the best prices came from the ones who grew their own oranges and grapefruits.

I had just gotten my driver's license (in those days you could drive alone at age 16), and I was able to drive by myself. I was no expert in fruit, and I was always concerned that the wholesaler would not give me the best fruit for the price we were paying. I would look over the bins of the oranges and grapefruits and try to pick the ones that had at least a week to mature before ripening. This would give us time to bag them, place them out front, and make a sale before they would start to spoil. I felt like we had a maximum of two weeks from the time we bought them until we could no longer sell them as fresh fruit.

One major problem I had was a lack of money. Numerous times, I tried to buy on credit, but I was not successful. Once we paid by check, but the check bounced, and from then on, we had to pay cash. I knew how much cash I had to spend (whatever Mother had given me), but the wholesalers did not. I would try to get the best price and the most oranges or the best-sized oranges that I could negotiate from the wholesaler, which offered the best deal. The only trick I could think of was to wait until late in the day when they were about to close to make my final choice, hoping they wanted to get rid of some more fruit that day because they too were worried about freshness. In any event, I drove home in the dark many times with a pickup truck full of the freshest oranges and grapefruit available that day.

Once back at the fruit shop, we would put the oranges into a tub of hot water filled with a wax solution. This slight film of wax would make the fruit shine and look more beautiful than their normal skins projected. Then we would bag them, place them out front on the sidewalk, and wait for a car to stop and buy. I loved the fresh orange juice and the meaty part that would float to the top of the container after squeezing. I would come home from football or basketball practice, gulp down a gallon of orange juice, and as needed, get in the pickup truck and go get more oranges. It took around four hours to get there, negotiate, and select the oranges and then drive home.

We were not hugely successful, but we did live off the fruit shop profits for two years until Mother decided to leave Daddy and Williston and move to Jacksonville with Robbie and Sara.

We did not have a radio in the old truck, and I had plenty of time to reflect on the art of negotiating. It was quite clear to me, then and now, that if you can create a product that another one needs, not just wants, you will also create a significant advantage.

# Chapter Thirty-Six

"Why did they do that to Whitey?" We were deer hunting in the Ocala National Forest with our horses and dogs.

The deer hunting in Gulf Hammock, our normal hunting grounds, had been terrible for a few years, so Uncle Oliver and Daddy had decided to try a new place. We had moved our tents, cooking equipment, sleeping bags and cots, dogs, horses, and groceries to the Ocala National Forest. It was only forty to fifty miles from Williston and not such a long drive for anyone who wanted to come over for a weekend. This was an unusual move for us. We normally hunted in areas we knew were only hunted by our family because we felt we had trained our family to hunt safely.

We had some success the first few days, and we were getting familiar with the area and beginning to understand how the deer moved and where they ran when chased by the dogs. The way we hunted is no longer allowed in many places, but it was common back then. The men would ride the horses with the dogs following them on horseback. The horsemen would take the dogs into an area where they suspected deer were living.

This process of hunting the deer is called a drive. The dogs would range out in front of the riders, and when they struck a deer trail, they would begin to bark. The first dog to bark would cause the rest of the dogs to come to him, and if they all caught the scent, the race would begin with a pack of dogs running after the trail of a deer. When they got near the deer, the deer would start running. If the drive was executed correctly, the riders would get a decent shot or the standers who had been placed in strategic locations in front of the drive would kill the deer (if it was a buck).

When a deer is running, it flashes its white tail, which can be seen far away and is much more visible than the deer itself. The flashing tail is often the first thing a hunter sees when the deer is running. The dogs would often get real close to the deer, and within moments of killing a deer, the dogs would be right there to partake of the kill. We would cut the deer's throat to let it bleed quickly and rid the muscles of blood to make the flavor better. The dogs would lick the blood and howl with delight. Once cleaned, we would give some deer meat and bones to the dogs. This would serve both as a treat and to train them to want more deer meat and to hunt better.

As you can see, the dogs and the deer were often in the same space when running through the woods. We all knew this, and when hunting, we were extremely careful not to shoot a dog. We were taught to never, never shoot at anything unless you know exactly what it is you are shooting. Do not ever shoot at a noise in the bushes or at something you just think is a deer!

Whitey, was one of our best hounds. He was a totally white dog except for a little brown on his head and ears. He had a strong, deep hunting voice and was always out in front of the pack. Well, this day, we made a successful drive and had an exciting chase, but no one from our camp killed the deer. We did hear some gunshots during the race, but none of our group had done the shooting. After the hunt, we called the dogs back to the dog wagon with bugles made of cow horns. We would blow on the horns with a distinctive sequence or melody. *Ba rup, ba rup, ba rup, ba ruppppppppp.* The dogs had been trained to come to this "bugle call," and we would load them in the dog pens in the back of available trucks to return to camp or to make another drive.

All the dogs returned to the horn blowing except Whitey. We went back to camp worried about Whitey but thinking he would find camp later, and maybe he was still out hunting by himself. He did not return that night. We had collars on all of our dogs with the name Brooks on them, and the game wardens had a list of those persons camping at the various sites in the forest, so they knew how to find us. Early the next morning, a game warden brought Whitey to the camp, dead. He was shot through the heart with a rifle; he must have died instantly.

We checked around and did not find anyone to admit to killing Whitey. We figured anyone dumb enough to either mistake a dog for a deer or mean enough to kill a dog was likely to shoot at horses as well. Since we were riding horses and did not want to lose any more dogs, we packed up and went back to Gulf Hammock to our familiar and safe hunting grounds. The Brooks family has hunted in that area for more than one hundred years and has never had a shooting accident nor ever killed a dog while hunting.

Even in business and life, unless you are careful to identify your target or goal, you will not likely be successful, and it is possible that you will also hurt others in the process.

# Chapter Thirty-Seven

"What is that big thing in our mullet net?" We were seining for mullet in the Homosassa River just before it empties into the Gulf of Mexico. Homosassa is around fifty miles south of Williston. The river starts as a crystal clear spring, and after a short distance, it becomes stained with tannin and turns a dark shade of brown all the way to the Gulf. This river is a fisherman's paradise. A freshwater fisherman can catch bass, bream, catfish, and bluegill. A saltwater angler can catch sea trout, redfish, grouper, snapper, tarpon, and mullet. As the river dumps into the gulf, there are many saltwater flats and mangrove islands.

My father and Jake Newson were planning a fish fry for a large crowd, and we needed at least fifty to seventy-five fish to feed the guests. We were going for mullet, which are a tasty fish, and the best place to fish for them is along the gulf coast of Florida. The body of the mullet is long and rather stout with lots of yummy white meat. Mullet swim in large schools and are often spotted jumping out of the water as they swim along. They are vegetarian, and a strange fact is that they actually have a gizzard much like a chicken. When you find a school of mullet, you can certainly catch many fish fast.

You cannot often catch a mullet with a rod and reel, and the traditional method of harvesting mullet is with a cast net, a beach net, or a seine net. Our strategy was to stretch a seine net across a narrow offshoot of the river, which was near the mouth of the gulf. The net had weights on its bottom row to position it firmly on the mud bottom of the river. It also had floats to keep the top of the net on the top of the water. Therefore, with the net stretched from one side to the other of the narrow waterway and with the net resting on the bottom, we had a barrier to stop any fish swimming through this passage. The tide was falling toward the gulf, and the fish were leaving the shallow river area to go out to the deeper waters of the gulf.

We saw the mullet hitting the net, and we knew we were going to have a fantastic catch when we pulled in the net. Everyone was excited, especially me, because we were catching so many fish so fast. The mullet were jumping out of the water, and we were whooping and hollering with glee. Then, something big hit the net; the net sagged beneath the water, and some of the mullet jumped over the net and escaped. Then it hit the net repeatedly. We were afraid to go into the water because we thought it might be a shark. We were also afraid we were going to lose the mullet and that the net would be destroyed. Finally, Jake took his .38 pistol, waded into the water, and started shooting at the gray shadow as it swirled around the net again and again.

I do not know how many times he had fired the pistol before we saw blood, and the big thing stopped hitting the net. We still did not know what it was because it did not float to the top. We pulled in the net, and along with more than one hundred mullet was a large dead tarpon. I had never seen such a big fish before, and my father thought most people in our town had never seen one either. He took the tarpon to town, hung it from a tree next to the town park, and it attracted a huge number of people. The tarpon weighed 120 pounds and was a beautiful fish.

We had a rollicking fish fry and a robust and long-winded conversation about the tarpon: brave Jake wading into the river without knowing what he was going to encounter, shooting at an unknown shadow, hitting a swirling target, and getting back on the shore alive. I have fished many ways for tarpon since that time and have caught them on spin tackle, bait-casting reels, and on fly.

However, I must say that my first tarpon catch, at age 11, was with a .38 pistol and a net—a fact that not many anglers can use in their fish stories.

# Chapter Thirty-Eight

"Let's go frog gigging." Terry, Butch, and I decided to go frog gigging one night.

Fried frog legs are a real tasty treat, and the ponds around the farm were filled with bullfrogs and pig frogs. The bullfrog is a large, bulky frog, and they can grow as big as two pounds and be almost one foot long. The pig frog is similar to the bullfrog except it is a little bit slimmer than the bullfrog and darker in color with freckles on its face.

The frog gig is essentially a small spear with three, four, or five barbed prongs on the tip. The pole should be twelve to fifteen feet long. You need a headlamp that holds tightly to your head and one that gives a strong, bright beam. You can wade around the shoreline of the ponds, but we preferred to gig from a small wooden boat. Gigging is also hunting, and you need to move slowly and look carefully at lily pads, the thick grass patches, and limbs in the water to locate the frogs sitting on them. It is not as easy as you might think to see the two eyes reflecting back at you or the white under their throats. Once you find a frog, you must approach slowly and keep the light shining in his eyes. Then you spear the frog, put him in the boat in some ice, and look for another. Sometimes when you looked for frogs, you would spot an alligator's eyes; and unless you want an unpleasant situation, you move along and leave him alone.

Well, we gigged around twenty-five nice frogs and decided we had enough. We came back to Uncle Oliver's house, and in the backyard, we cleaned the frogs. We removed the frogs' legs with an extremely sharp knife and tossed the rest of the frog into a burlap bag. Once we finished, we put the burlap bag on the back porch to throw away the next day and put the freshly cleaned frog legs in the icebox. We were planning on a feast the next night when Aunt Dorothy would prepare the frog legs for us along with grits with melted cheese.

We three went to bed around midnight. Awakened with screams early the next morning, we jumped out of bed. Aunt Dorothy was yelling that there were frogs all over the house. The frogs we had put in the burlap were not dead as we had thought but were dragging their dismembered bodies around the house leaving a mess. Aunt Dorothy was furious at seeing such a mess, and we spent a lot of time with mops, brushes, and soapy water cleaning and recleaning the linoleum floor of her house. We stayed away from Aunt Dorothy the rest of that day and most of the night, and I don't think we ever got to eat those frog legs.

# Chapter Thirty-Nine

"Kay, let me show you something pretty." My cousin Kay Warren lived in Ocala with the rest of the Gerald clan, who were my mother's parents, sisters, brothers-in-law, nieces, and nephews. Ocala was a large city compared to Montbrook.

We would sometime visit Ocala on a Sunday to eat with mother's family. Ocala was about twenty-five miles from Williston, and it had fancy stores, beautiful homes, and many restaurants. I was around seven years old, and we were still living on the farm when we took one of our trips to eat and visit with them.

I never paid much attention to the route we took to get to Granny Gerald's house or the street on which she and Grandpa Gerald lived. Kay was two years older than me and had lived in Ocala all of her life. She knew her way around the town. Kay asked me to go to a little grocery store with her, which was not too far away, to get some ingredients they needed for cooking. After we bought the stuff and started home, unknown to me, Kay decided to leave me behind as a trick. She told me to wait for a minute on a corner, and she would be right back, but she did not come back. I had no idea how to get back to Granny's house. I ran in a bunch of different directions, but none of them looked familiar. I was dreadfully scared and did not know what to do.

Finally, I went up to the door of a strange house and knocked softly. A lady came to the door and asked me what I wanted. I asked her if she knew how to get to Granny's house. She did not know what Granny I was talking about. She asked me what street Granny lived on, and I started to cry because I did not know. The lady was patient, and finally, she got the name Gerald from me, looked up the name in her phone book, called the number, and my mother came to get me. I never forgave Kay for that trick, and I decided to seek revenge when I had the opportunity.

About three months later, Kay and her parents came to visit us at the farm. We had lunch together, and Kay and I went out to play in the yard. Our farmhouse yard was several acres, and behind the house were the barn and some other outbuildings. There were lots of room to run and play and many things to explore. Just behind the barn were a large number of giant oak trees with hanging moss and air plants growing on the big limbs. I told Kay that I had seen something super unusual that I wanted to show her. It was a gray cone hanging from one of the limbs and not very high up in the tree. I told Kay that it was something so special that we should knock it down with some rocks and take it to the house because her parents would really be impressed that we had found such a thing. I found a dozen or so rocks and placed them in a pile on the ground. I told Kay she could go first, and I would get a bucket to put the cone in after she knocked it down.

Well, Kay started throwing one rock after another at the cone, and all of a sudden, a number of highly angry hornets started flying out of the cone directly for Kay. I knew what was going to happen, so I had hidden behind a large tree, far away from the activity. Only one hornet bit her, but that was enough. Hornets are among the meanest of all wasps, and their sting is particularly strong. As expected and as there should have been, there was crying, wailing, anger, and punishment directed at me.

I got in real trouble for my revenge, but Kay never lost me again when we visited the family in Ocala.

# Chapter Forty

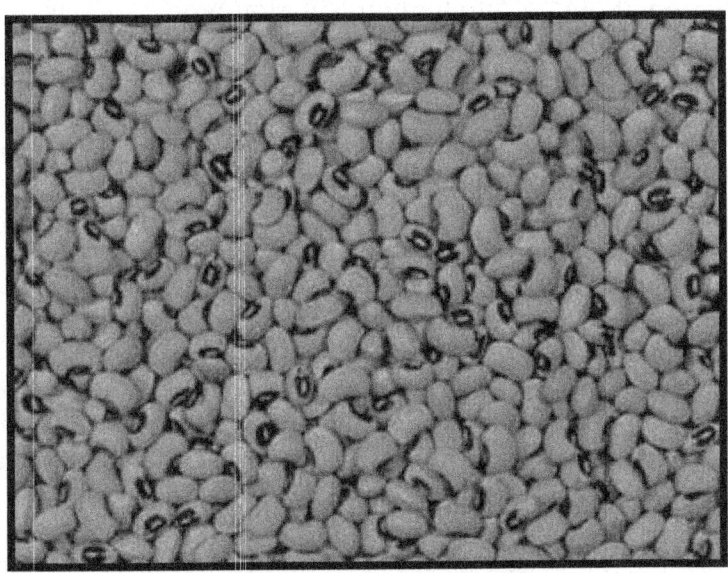

"Run, Pinky, run." It was high noon, and we were hot and thirsty when Grandpa Brooks finally arrived in the pea field. Cousin Baker, Carl "Pinky" Pinkston, and I had been picking black-eyed peas in the North Morgan field for several hours since we had enjoyed our last drink of water. It was one hundred degrees in the sun, and we were working in the field with no hats. We had accidentally spilled the cooler of water Grandpa had left with us. He had dropped us off around 10:00 a.m. and told us to pick a few bushels of black-eyed peas for eating and canning. We were extremely eager for him to arrive with a drink of water.

Black-eyed peas are grown around the world for food. I think they initially came from India and were first planted in Virginia in the 1600s. They found their way to Florida a century later. In Texas, they call them

Texas caviar. We loved to eat them, and all the women in the family would can as much as possible during the harvest season to enjoy throughout the year.

Our refrigeration was limited and canning was a safe method of food preservation if practiced properly—a skill that our family had learned long ago. The process involved placing the peas (or other vegetables) in jars and heating them to a temperature that killed everything that could make you sick or cause the food to spoil. When the jar is heated, air is removed; and as it cools, a vacuum seal is formed. This vacuum prevents air from getting back into the peas and bringing with it any organisms that could recontaminate the food.

We saw Grandpa coming on the tractor pulling a flatbed trailer on which we would ride back to his house in Montbrook. We yelled at each other to race to where Grandpa would stop the tractor. Baker and I were always faster than Pinky, and we always ragged on him for being so slow compared to us. He just did not seem to be able to run fast, and we did not know why, but we always outran him. So Baker and I won the race and teased Pinky again about how slow he was.

Grandpa had brought some new cold water with him, and we gulped it down in huge quantities. We were also hungry and could hardly wait to have lunch at Mema's table. It was about a thirty-minute ride to the house, and as we got about halfway home, we three had to pee badly to get rid of some of the excess water we had consumed. Grandpa could not hear us over the sound of the tractor, so we decided to jump off the trailer while it was still moving, do our business and then run to catch up with the trailer. If we were fast, Grandpa would not even know we left the trailer.

When we were finished, Baker and I started running as fast as we could run, and we caught up with the trailer, jumped on board, and looked back to see Pinky eating the dust. We were just passing the Sistrunk Lake, and Pinky was not making much progress in catching up with the moving vehicle. Baker suddenly yelled out, "Pinky, there is a black panther coming out of the lake, and he's going to eat you if he catches you."

All of a sudden, Pinky started running at a speed that we had never seen him perform. Baker had created a moment of real motivation for Pinky. Pinky quickly caught the trailer, and he was never slow again. In all future races, Pinky was right there with the winners including his later business life.

Sometimes, it takes a special moment to bring out the best in all of us.

## Chapter Forty-One

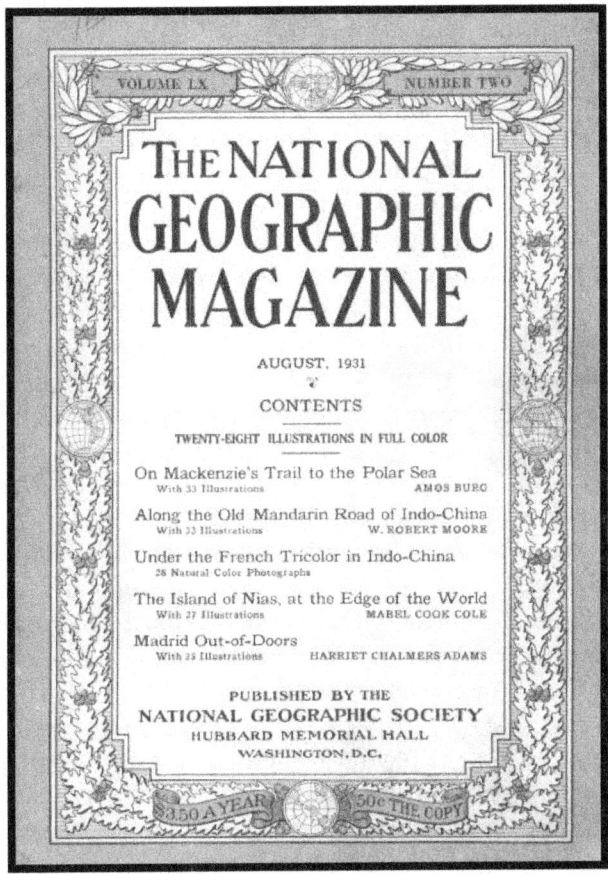

"Wow, I would like to go there someday!" Grandpa Brooks had an extensive library of *National Geographic Magazines*. His collection started in the late 1800s and contained almost every issue published until his death in the 1950s. There are twelve issues per year, and so you can imagine how many copies there were to study and scan in utter amazement. This was before TV, and they were our first reliable glimpse of a larger world. We did see some of the world through the movies but not the in-depth view explained in the magazines.

According to their website, "The *National Geographic Magazine*, later shortened to *National Geographic*, published its first issue (October 1888) nine months after the Society was founded as the Society's official journal. The magazine has had for many years a trademarked yellow border around the edge of its cover. Gardiner Greene Hubbard became its first president and his son-in-law, Alexander Graham Bell, eventually succeeded him in 1897 following his death."

Grandpa kept the magazines stored in the old church building next to his rock house. His still existing distinctive rock house was built with rocks picked up from the area around the farm, and a long line of relatives has since lived in it.

The church had not been active for years and was used as a warehouse by Grandpa. Baker, Butch, and I would spend hours looking over the *National Geographic Magazines* and imagine ourselves in those exotic, faraway places. We learned geography, and we learned about the different ways that people look and live all over the world. We saw animals of all kinds for the first time, and we observed many different types of clothing and uniforms worn by different peoples in faraway places. We learned about mountains, oceans, and the creatures that live on and in them.

There was a large church bell high in the belfry with a rope still hanging down for years, but we were not allow to pull it. The former Baptist church, which had never been used in my childhood, still created an ambiance of reverence when we entered.

Between the reverence created by the church and the wondrous revelations we uncovered from reading, studying, and commenting about the *National Geographic Magazine*, we experienced an exceptional learning experience. Sometimes, Grandpa would visit us in the church and sit with us and explain the new things we were learning. It was a memorable time indeed.

During my adult life, I have travelled to many of the places we read about as youngsters, and rarely have I failed to think of the old church, the magazines, my cousins, and our first exposure to the world beyond the farm. I am convinced it gave us rural Brooks kids a more worldly view than most of our contemporaries.

# Chapter Forty-Two

"The kitty is dead." I ran back inside the farmhouse to tell my mother that the kitty had killed a snake, and that the snake had killed the kitty. They were both lying dead on our front porch, and I almost stepped on them as I went running out to play.

We had quite a few cats running more or less wild on our farm. Once in a while, we would put out some food for them, but mainly, they survived on the things they could catch and kill such as birds, rats, mice, baby rabbits, lizards, and snakes. There were plenty of rats and mice to kill and eat in the barns and outbuildings on the farm. In fact, one of the main reasons we kept the cats were for them to keep the rat and mice populations under control.

Genetics have given the cat family a lot of smart, confidence, and speed that make them excellent hunters. They are conditioned to think about hunting from the time they are born, and they start hunting and playing games that teach them to hunt from an early age. They not only watch their parents make a kill, but they are constantly playing, running, jumping, rolling over, swinging at objects with their paws, pouncing on items, sprinting from place to place, learning to fight by playing with their littermates, slinking, crouching, moving slowly, and learning to bite very skillfully with their razor-sharp teeth. In short, they are little killing machines remarkably early in their lives.

We had many types of snakes on our farm, and six of them were poisonous: eastern diamondback rattlesnakes, copperheads, cottonmouth moccasins, coral snakes, and pigmy rattlers. There are over forty species of snakes in Florida, and many are harmless, but not all.

I guess the kitty thought the brightly colored coral snake was harmless, but she was mistaken. Perhaps the snake bit the kitty and then she got angry and killed the snake with a hard bite to the head.

Another lesson to be learned: not all pretty things are harmless.

# Chapter Forty-Three

**MOST INTELLIGENT**
NANCY LEWIS
BAKER BROOKS

**BEST LOOKING**
NAOMI CHEELY
BOBBY SANDLIN

**MOST LIKELY TO SUCCEED**
GAIL WOMER
ALAN BROOKS

"I am extremely proud of my selection as 'Most Likely to Succeed.'" Our high school yearbook gave some superlatives to a few of our graduates. As soon as I knew that one had been given to me, I ran home and told my mother how proud I was to get that designation.

Baker Brooks and Nancy Lewis were voted the most intelligent. Baker became a farmer, insurance sales agent, and horse breeder. Nancy became a librarian. Bobby Sandlin (he and I were born on the same day, month, and year) and Naomi Cheely were voted the best looking. Bobby became a pharmacist and businessman. Naomi became a housewife, and I am not sure of her professional life. Gail Womer and I were voted "Most Likely to Succeed." Gail married Bobby Bullock, and they travelled around the world with Bobby's profession. I am not sure of Gail's professional life. I recently saw all the above classmates, except Nancy Lewis, at a fiftieth class reunion and thoroughly enjoyed catching up on some of the details of their lives.

I went through all twelve grades with these classmates, and I knew them well. It was such a wonderful environment to know your classmates for so long and to be friends with most of them for years and years. A large percentage of our graduating class started together in the first grade, and most of us who started together did graduate together.

Baker, Naomi, and Bobby still live in the Williston area. Gail, Nancy, and I all moved away and did not live our adult lives in the area we were born and raised. I think more than half of our graduating class (around forty in the class) stayed in the Williston area. When I moved away, I lost contact with most of them. Even when I went back to visit, I only saw a few of them. I think of them often but have not maintained a close relationship with any of them except Baker and Butch.

I have often thought about this superlative that was given to me. I think it motivated me to strive harder many times when things were not going so smoothly as an adult. I wanted to live up to the promise this designation held out as a possibility for me to achieve.

Success is a many-faceted idea, and I often reflected on what I would need to do to be considered a success by my classmates and myself. I have come to believe that success is the following: achieving a college education (and beyond); maintaining a solid spousal relationship; raising loving children who become responsible citizens; working at something you enjoy and, if possible, something you have created; accumulating enough money to see the world and retire with only reasonable financial worries; interacting with grandchildren who have the same values as their loving and responsible parents; contributing money and time to some charities; having some fun hobbies; and having faith in God.

If my definition is accurate, then I did as my classmates predicted; I succeeded!

# Chapter Forty-Four

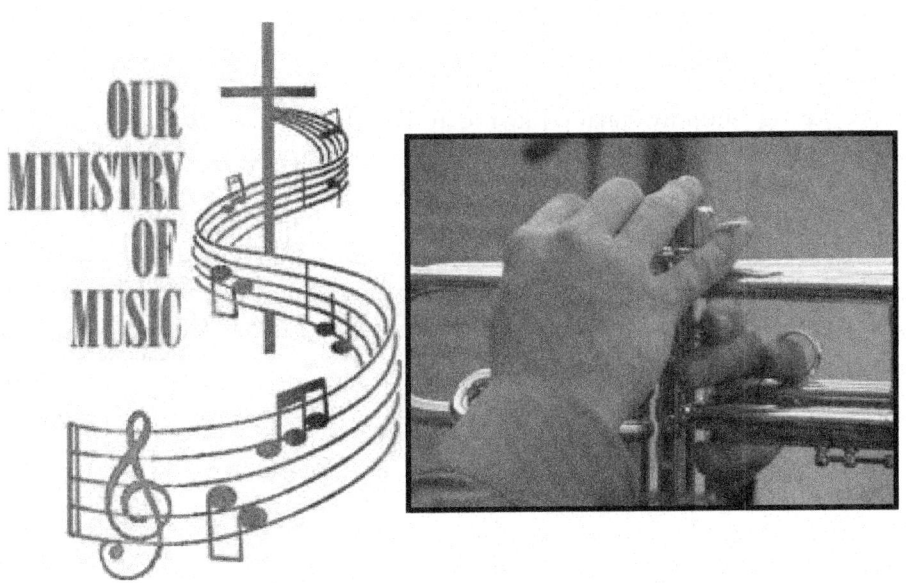

"Let's play 'Amazing Grace.'" Danny Fletcher, Leone Sapp, and I played in our high school band. Danny and Leone played clarinets, and I played a trumpet. Danny was the first chair in the clarinet section, Leone was second chair, and I was the first chair in the trumpet section of the band. We were all proud of our skills.

We were all three Baptists, and we were frequently asked to play hymns as part of the Sunday services at the Williston First Baptist Church. Most of the time we would be accompanied by Ms. Smith, who played the piano and organ.

The Williston First Baptist Church was comprised of several old redbrick buildings that included the main sanctuary plus some adjacent rooms for Sunday school and the administrative offices. The main sanctuary could hold a few hundred people, and it was not often full except for Easter and Christmas services.

The Baptists and the Methodists are both Christian religions. In my childish understanding, the main difference was the method of being baptized and who could be baptized. The Methodists sprinkled water on the head of the person to be baptized while the Baptists believe in full-body immersion in a pool of water. The Methodists would baptize children while the Baptists would only baptize young people capable of understanding the Baptist faith. In general, Baptists are considered more fundamentalist than Methodist. My mother's family were Methodists, and my father's family were Baptists. There was often heated debate over the virtues of each religious affiliation.

We played many of the old classic Baptist hymns: "Amazing Grace," "The Old Rugged Cross," "What a Friend We Have in Jesus," "Onward Christian Soldiers," "Nearer My God to Thee," and many others. We were young when we started playing at the church, and some of our early music included missed notes and off-tune sections. As we grew in age and skills, our musical talents improved, and we were a highly popular part of many Sunday morning services for a number of years.

It is fun and educational to play music, and I think learning the notations and logic of music helps a young person develop an appreciation for organized thinking—the need for practice also develops discipline and diligence.

# Chapter Forty-Five

"Run or he will whip you with his tail!" The Florida coachwhip snake is the fastest snake I have ever seen. It is also a large snake that will normally be five to eight feet in length. They like to raise their heads to look around for something to eat, and they are extremely aggressive.

Some people say it got its name from the tapered tail, which looks like a whip. I was told, and I believe, that it got its name from the pleasure it takes in whipping small children who it can outrun. The authorities say it loves the sandhill areas, palmetto thickets, and even the dunes along the Florida beaches. I have never seen one in those areas, but I can tell you, as a certain fact, that they love blackberry bushes. I know because one of the fencerows along the North Morgan field had enormous clumps of blackberry bushes.

We loved nothing more than Aunt Dorothy's blackberry doobie. She would take the fresh blackberries that we picked, add sugar, water, some cornstarch, and butter to create a mixture. While the mixture of juice was simmering, she would make dumplings from flour, sugar, and vegetable shortening. Then she put the dumplings into the simmering liquid and berries and let it cook for around one-half hour. The smell was so tantalizing that the muscles in your jaws would start working, and your taste buds would do a dance like an Irish jig.

She could get all the ingredients at the local grocery except the fresh blackberries; that was our job. So we had real motivation to get the berries even with the fear of the coachwhip snake that we knew lived in those bushes. We called him (we always said him, but I am not sure) Speedy. We hoped we were fast enough to outrun Speedy, even carrying a bucket of berries, but none of us was convinced that we were fast enough. On several occasions, we were chased by Speedy and had barely escaped without a whipping.

You can imagine the conflict between the pleasures of doobie versus the fear of Speedy. Each time, we approached the bushes with great care, picking a few berries, studying the ground under the bushes for signs of Speedy, readying our feet to move back from the bushes quickly, and readying to run at a moment's notice.

Speedy never whipped any of us, but there was no doubt that he would whip us if he could catch us. Overcoming fear of things both real and imagined is difficult, but it is often necessary to reach your goals.

# Chapter Forty-Six

Marble Time.

"That does not hurt so much." Like most of my classmates, I started going to school in the first grade. The elementary school was adjacent to the high school, and each had a separate playground area.

We had several breaks during the day plus our lunch hour. A few of the boys in my class liked to play marbles, and we were almost obsessed with the game in the third and fourth grades. We needed a small dirt area that had a level surface so that we could draw a circle in the ground with a pointed stick. We would decide how many marbles we wanted to wager and then each player would place his marbles in the circle.

The object of the game was to keep your fingers outside of the circle (on your first shot) using a "shooter" marble to hit the marbles in the circle and knock at least one of them out of the circle ring. If you knocked at least one marble out of the circle and your "shooter" marble stayed in the circle, you could keep shooting as long as each shot knocked another marble out of the circle. Each player could keep the marbles he knocked out of the circle—we called this type of marble game "for keeps." A skilled player might knock all the marbles out of the circle during his first turn. Teachers did not like us to play "for keeps."

Once we had the circle drawn and the marbles in the circle, we needed to determine who would go first and have the best chance at getting the most marbles. We created a lag line in the sand about ten feet away from a baseline. Each player would toss a special, heavy marble used especially for lagging at the lag line. The player who got the closest to the "lag line" would go first; the player who was second closest would go second, and so forth.

One day we were playing "for keeps," and a new kid wanted to join us. We all put in twelve marbles, made our lag, and he came in last. Two of us knocked all the marbles out of the circle before he even had a turn. He was mad and embarrassed that he had lost his marbles.

When we returned to the classroom, he told the teacher we had stolen his marbles. We denied this allegation, but the teacher felt she should make an example of us for playing marbles "for keeps." She used a ping-pong paddle to spank us in front of the class. We had to bend over, and she hit us on the butt a couple of times—not very hard.

It was embarrassing, but no physical damage occurred, and there were no complaints from my parents. It is crucial that teachers maintain discipline, and a harmless little paddle can achieve big results. We stopped playing "for keeps."

# Chapter Forty-Seven

"Daddy, here comes one, low over the trees." Our entire family loved to bird hunt. We hunted dove, quail, and duck on the farm and in the state hunting preserve called Gulf Hammock.

We planted corn and peanuts on the farm as crops to sell and to feed the farm animals. After the farm equipment harvested the corn and peanuts, many fragments of them would be lying on the ground and easy for the dove to see and eat. The dove hunting regulations permitted hunting from noon to sunset during the allowed seasons of the year. We would hunt in the harvested fields starting around 1:00 in the afternoon and hunt until dark.

The correct name of the doves we hunted is mourning dove. They are super fast and can fly up to fifty miles per hour, which makes it a challenge to hit them with a gun. If the wind is blowing, the dove can turn to another direction so fast that it is incredible. Their speed and maneuverability is what makes dove hunting such a fun sport, and they are good to eat.

One of the dove seasons started in September; it could be extremely hot, and we needed to dress for the heat. Some of us had camouflage shirts, but it was so hot we often wore no shirts at all. We found any cover we could find to hide behind such as fencerows, trees, and bushes. Doves can see exceptionally well, and they will flare away if you are in the open or make any movement when they are flying in your direction.

We used shotguns with number 8 shot. We used a variety of shotgun models: 410 gauges, 16 gauges, and 12 gauges. It is imperative to learn some safety and courtesy rules when one starts to hunt dove: never shoot on the level, which could hit another hunter; never kill more than your limit (normally twelve per day); never get close to another hunter, who is in a great spot to share in his shooting; and never drink alcohol while hunting.

Doves visit a water hole around sunset to quench their thirst before their nightly roosting in the trees. A water hole is a fantastic spot to end the day of hunting. The sun is setting, painting the sky orange and pink, the dove come in fast and furious, diving, turning, alighting for just a brief moment, flying away, and darting constantly. A hunter must be exceedingly careful if there are other hunters at the water hole because the doves fly so low it is tempting to shoot on the level as the birds dive to get a drink.

We had many fabulous times hunting doves. My father was the best shot of all the family members, and I was so proud to see him shoot during the hunt. He rarely missed, and all would marvel at how far away he could hit a bird no matter how quickly they were flying or how much they darted.

We cleaned the birds immediately after the hunt, and they were cooked and on our plates within a short time. Served with grits, gravy, and biscuits, they make a real treat. What a meal!

# Chapter Forty-Eight

"I want that BB gun so badly." There were a few stores in Williston that I remember so well: the Western Auto Store, the 5 and Dime, Barton's Grocery Store, the Blizzard Shop, the Movie Theater, and the Barber Shop.

The Western Auto store had all kinds of guns. When I was around eight years old, I had a huge desire to get a BB gun that looked like a real Winchester repeating rifle. There were several displayed in the window, and any time we went to town, I would drool over them and beg my parents to buy me one. The owners knew my parents, and they would let me hold and aim the BB gun that I truly wanted. Eventually, my parents gave me the one I wanted on my ninth birthday. I practiced continuously, and soon, I was the best shot among my family and group of friends. Later when I was around twelve, they let me get a .22 rifle. I worked at many odd jobs (both on the farm and in town) to get money for ammunition. I continued to practice until I was super proficient, and years later when I was in the army, I won a large tournament as a shooter of several rifles.

There was one main grocery store in Williston owned by Edward Lee Barton. It was where we went to buy most of our staple items including meats when we had none at home. My parents had a "charge account," and when I went to get groceries, I would just say, "Charge it to Mother." They knew my parents, my uncles, and me. When I got groceries for Uncle Oliver, I would say, "Charge it to Uncle Oliver." They rarely said, "Tell your parents or uncle we need to see them about their bill," but occasionally I would carry that message home along with the groceries.

I loved a "blizzard" ice-cream concoction more than anything I can remember. As I previously mentioned, I also enjoy a strawberry soda with a moon pie. However, the "blizzard" was in a world all by itself: thick strawberry ice cream, gooey sweet walnuts, a variety of other toppings all jumbled together in a twenty-ounce cup. I think it costs twenty cents, maybe thirty cents. The movie was ten cents, ten cents for a drink, and five cents for a few Mary Jane's. Often, I had to choose between the blizzard and the movies since my Saturday allowance was usually twenty-five to fifty cents.

It is hard to believe, but in the 40s and 50s, the movie theater was segregated. Blacks were required to enter through the back door and sit upstairs while we entered through the front door and were seated downstairs. There was never any incident of any kind, but I always worried about how they must feel to be separated for no valid reason. The person who ran the movie projector did not have his full mental faculties, but he was such a nice fellow, and all liked him. He also managed the popcorn machine, which was downstairs, and the projector, which was upstairs. If he failed to start the next reel on time, the entire movie house would hoot and holler in a friendly way to encourage him to get back upstairs and fix the next reel.

Kindness and meanness existed side by side in that movie house.

# Chapter Forty-Nine

"Alan, are you planning to go to college?" Noah Long, a respected local citizen and the Federal Game Warden for the Central Florida area, knocked on the door of our little house when we were living in the back of the fruit shop.

This was an exceedingly bad time for our family, both financially and emotionally. Daddy was at his worst stage of drinking, unemployment, and home disturbance. I had always hoped to go to college, but there was absolutely no money available for me, and we did not possess the knowledge in our family to pursue scholarship money. At this point, I had no way to attend college when I graduated from high school.

Up until now, no one from our immediate Brooks family or cousins had received a college degree. My father had attended one year of college, but he dropped out when his father got tick fever that made him seriously ill for a long while. My sister Jo Ann attended a vocational business school and was a highly skilled bookkeeper living in Jacksonville. My cousin, Baker, was planning to attend UF in the fall.

I knew Mr. Long because he had taken me with him a few times on his rounds to the Ocala National Forest, local hunting fields, and the Gulf Hammock State hunting preserve that were part of his territory. He had also arranged for me to hunt on the property owned by Cecil Webb, who was the owner of Dixie Lily Grits.

Mr. Webb, a successful businessman, was one of the biggest employers in our town, and his grits were sold all over the south. Mr. Webb was also a Florida State cabinet officer, secretary of transportation. He had a large farm and had imported pheasants and ducks to his property to create a unique hunting experience. He placed hunting blinds all over his property in which his guests would hide. He would release the pheasants and ducks one at a time, and as they would attempt to fly away, the hunters would shoot them. I never thought this was so sporting, but people from all over the state and the world wanted a chance to hunt with Mr. Webb and experience his southern hospitality of hunting, drinking, eating, and storytelling. It was a real treat to be included in this experience.

Mr. Long asked if he could come into our house, and my mother said yes. He asked to see me, and when I went into the kitchen, my mother, my father, and Mr. Long were seated at our small kitchen table. He told us that a group of local civic clubs had put together money for me to attend the University of Florida. The Masons, Pythian Sisters, and the Kiwanis Club were going to donate enough money each semester to pay my tuition and housing. I would need to work to pay for my food, books, and other expenses, but the tuition and housing would be covered by the town scholarship.

My mother was extremely excited, and I was stunned with both surprise and pride that the townsfolk would think of me in such a way. My father, who had been drinking heavily, told Mr. Long that we did not need any financial help and asked him to leave the house. Mr. Long did as asked, and he left the house.

I went out into the street, running after him, begging him not to listen to my father, telling him that I would welcome the money, explaining that I was so grateful and assuring him that I would do an excellent job as a university student. They did as promised, and I attended the university in the fall of 1958 with exactly the amount of money needed to pay my tuition and housing.

My mother, bless her heart, gave me the only extra money she had ($5) when she dropped me off at school with a few clothes in a paper bag, tears in my eyes, and a lot of hope in my heart. Within fifteen minutes, I had a job working as a kitchen helper in the cafeteria where I worked to earn my food and book money.

Essentially, my rural childhood was over.

The photograph shown above is my formal high school graduation picture.

# Additional Items about the Area and the Family

Maps of the area

Montbrook (where the farms were located) is four miles south of Williston, which is in Levy County, Florida. Levy County was created in 1845. It was named for David Levy, the first member of the United States Senate and a practicing Jew. Levy was also one of Florida's first two US senators and served from 1845 to 1851 and again from 1855 to 1861. Levy also constructed the first railroad in Florida linking the ports of Cedar Key on the Gulf of Mexico to Fernandina on the Atlantic Ocean.

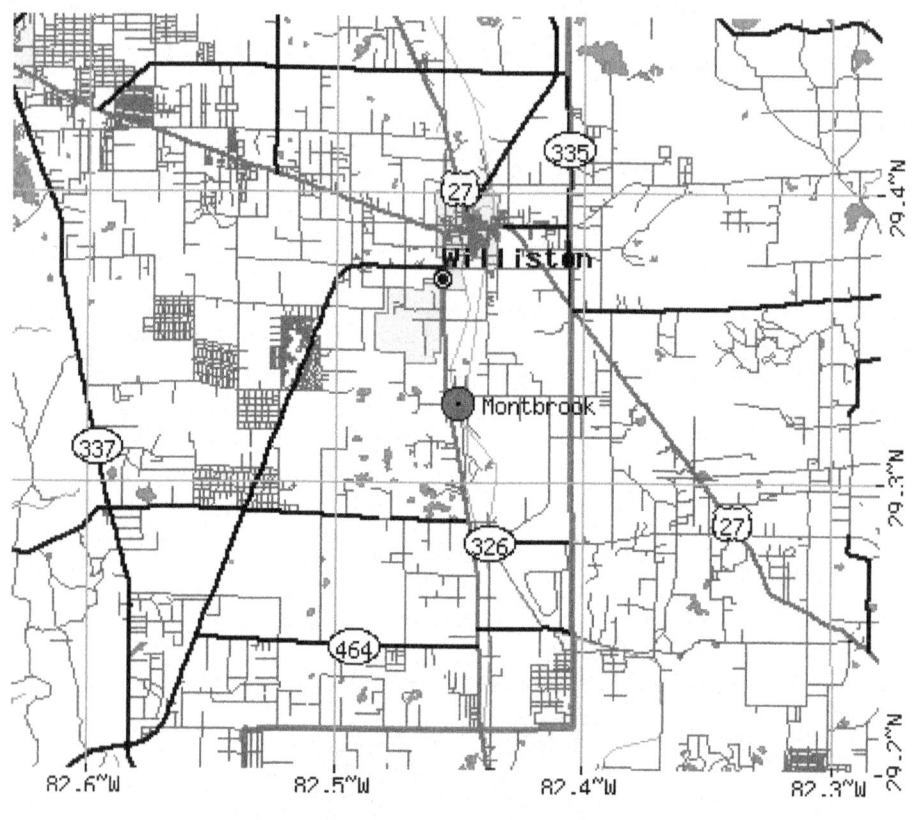

Montbrook facts from research and the internet (*FLGenWeb Project, Inc.*)

a. The little town finally became Montbrook, Florida, (named in honor of Montholon Brooks) on July 22, 1899. Montholon Brooks married Mary Plummer in 1877 and was a farmer by profession.
b. Prior to 1892, when the town was known as Phoenix Heights, it became known as Ambler, probably named for the lumber and timber baron, D. C. Ambler of Ambler & Taliaferro Lumber Company in business from 1889 to 1900.
c. The 1911–1912 edition of the R. L. Polk & Company's "Florida Gazeteer & Business Directory" states the following: Montbrook had a population of 481, had Baptist & Methodist Episcopal Churches, had a public school, had two sawmills, Mayor was Daniel Linbough, Marshal was A. G. McDonald.
d. The 1918 edition of the R. L. Polk & Company's "Florida Gazeteer & Business Directory" states the following: Montbrook had a population of five hundred, had Baptist and a Methodist Churches, a hotel named *the Davis Hotel* owned and operated by J. R. Davis, three general stores, a barber, a meat store, a livery stable, a drug store, and The Florida Land Company (sawmill & naval stores). At this point, Montbrook was bigger than Williston.
e. In 1925, it shows a population of 250, and the town consisted of the above mentioned plus a notary of the Veneer & Basket Company, a livery stable, five livestock breeders, and a ties and post company. I think this is when the sawmills burned down and the businesses left the area.
f. The Plummer Cemetery is located on Route 41 just southwest of Montbrook. This is where most of the Brooks families are buried.
g. The Montbrook Post Office was located on a piece of property just a few yards down from where the Davis Hotel stood. Miss Emily Sneller became postmistress in 1915 when her father Peter Otto Sneller turned seventy years old and served until the town burned out due to a fire in the sawmill, and the mails began coming through the Williston Post Office. The Montbrook Post Office was disestablished on September 30, 1955.
h. Peter Otto Sneller's other daughter, Miss Agnes Sheffield, was the Montbrook schoolteacher and was adored by all.
i. In the early days, Montbrook was bigger than Williston and ran all the way to Morriston on Route 41.
j. The source is Fl-genweb.org (FLGenWeb Project, Inc.).

# Florida Brooks Family History

Montholon (Mont) Brooks was born on October 4, 1854, at Brooksville, Florida, and he died on July 3, 1929. According to my great-aunt Nettie (a daughter of Montholon) who wrote a history of our family in 1962, his grandparents (we do not know their given names) came to Florida by oxcart in the same group as Osceola's parents. Osceola became a very famous Seminole Indian chief. Both families settled on the Hillsboro River, near what is now Tampa, Florida. The Indians settled on one side of the river, and the Brooks family on the other. The city of Tampa was first called Ft. Brooks named for Montholon's grandfather. His grandfather had two sons, Oliver and Tom. Oliver moved to what is now Brooksville, Florida, and the town was later named for him. Oliver died young and left his wife and two children: a boy named Montholon and a girl named Amanda. Mont settled twenty miles northwest of Ocala, Florida, in 1877.

He was one of the early growers of the Seedling Orange. He also discovered phosphate on his land, which he used to grow his oranges. Later learning the value of the phosphate, he went into the business of mining and was the first man to mine the phosphate in Florida. It was through the efforts of Mont that the Seaboard Railroad Company built the tracks from Archer to Dunellon, Florida. He gave the right-of-way that split his plantation in half and then he made it into a town also donating the site for a railroad station. Later the town was named Montbrook for him, and it remains so until this day.

Montholon was married to Mary Jane Plummer who was born August 29, 1859, and died November 9, 1943. Her grandfather's parents were early Dutch immigrants who settled in Pennsylvania, where he was born. Her grandmother was born in New York. After they had married, they moved to Barnwell, South Carolina. They had one son, Joe Plummer (born 1829). Their South Carolina home was burned during the Civil War. Joe had moved to Florida when he was very young and was hired as an overseer on a plantation on the St. John's River near Palatka, Florida. While working there, he met his wife, Prudence Hale. Peter Hale was her father, and they had a large plantation near what is now Ocala, Florida. Peter was from Virginia, was the captain of a British vessel, and travelled widely. Joe Plummer and Prudence Hale had Mary Jane Plummer, who later married Montholon. Joe joined the Confederate army during the Civil War and later drew a pension until he died.

Montholon and Mary Jane had nine children. One of the children was Robert Luther Brooks, my grandfather, who was born in 1881 and died 1961. He married Ada Gornto (Mema) who was born in 1888 and died in 1980. Grandpa and Mema had Eugenia, Robert Jr. (Bob, my father), Joe, Oliver, Nellie, and Louise. Grandpa and Mema lived their entire lives on the land settled by Montholon. Joe was killed in the war. Nellie and Aunt Gene moved away with their families. Oliver and Aunt Louise also stayed on the farmland their entire lives. My father stayed in the area until 1958, then moved to Jacksonville and then returned to live on the farm with mother for the last ten years of their lives. Mother was born in 1912 and died in 1987. Daddy was born in 1911 and died in 1984.

Most of the Brooks family mentioned above are buried in the Plummer Cemetery near Montbrook, Florida.

# Florida Gerald History

Bert Cornelius Gerald (Grandpa Gerald) was born in 1886 and died December 9, 1952. Sally Strickland Gerald (Granny Gerald) was born 1892 and died August 7, 1966. Grandpa was born in Mullins, South Carolina, and Granny was born in Zoan, South Carolina.

They were married at Tabor City, North Carolina. They had four girls and one boy: Rubye (my mother), Helen, Estelle, Bert Jr. and Sadie. The family moved to Oxford, Florida, in 1917, and they spent their lives in the area of Oxford, Williston, and Ocala. Buddy Gerald farmed, raised tomatoes and watermelons, and operated a livestock brokerage business for horses and mules.

Grandpa and Granny are buried at Pine Level Cemetery in Oxford, Florida.

Rubye (my mother) had four children: Jo Ann, Alan, Robbie, and Sara.

Helen married Livingston Anderson, and they have three sons: Vann, Jerry, and Andy.

Estelle married Perry Warren, and they had one daughter, Kay. Perry died in 1942. Estelle married John Deen, and they had one daughter, Suzy.

Sadie married Charles Appleton, and they had two daughters: Steffany and Beth. Sadie married Gaylon Howe in 1980.

CPSIA information can be obtained
at www.ICGtesting.com
Printed in the USA
BVOW04*0603251116
468582BV00008B/19/P

9 781465 336842